CAMBRIDGE LIBRARY COLLECTION

Books of enduring scholarly value

Egyptology

The large-scale scientific investigation of Egyptian antiquities by Western scholars began as an unintended consequence of Napoleon's invasion of Egypt during which, in 1799, the Rosetta Stone was discovered. The military expedition was accompanied by French scholars, whose reports prompted a wave of enthusiasm that swept across Europe and North America resulting in the Egyptian Revival style in art and architecture. Increasing numbers of tourists visited Egypt, eager to see the marvels being revealed by archaeological excavation. Writers and booksellers responded to this growing interest with publications ranging from technical site reports to tourist guidebooks and from children's histories to theories identifying the pyramids as repositories of esoteric knowledge. This series reissues a wide selection of such books. They reveal the gradual change from the 'tomb-robbing' approach of early excavators to the highly organised and systematic approach of Flinders Petrie, the 'father of Egyptology', and include early accounts of the decipherment of the hieroglyphic script.

The Royal Tombs of the First Dynasty

A pioneering Egyptologist, Sir William Matthew Flinders Petrie (1853–1942) excavated over fifty sites and trained a generation of archaeologists. His meticulous recording of artefacts and his sequence dating of pottery types found in Egypt and Palestine made Near Eastern archaeology a more rigorous and scientific discipline. This fully illustrated report of 1900 on the royal tombs at Abydos, capital of Upper Egypt, covers the first dynasty (*c.*3100–*c.*2900 BCE). Although Petrie acknowledges that it is only a preliminary report of ongoing work, he gives detailed descriptions of six tombs and the associated finds. A chapter on the inscriptions is provided by Francis Llewellyn Griffith (1862–1934). Petrie wrote prolifically throughout his long career for both specialists and non-specialists. His follow-up report, *The Royal Tombs of the Earliest Dynasties* (1901), and the three-part *Abydos* (1902–4) are among those works also reissued in this series.

The Royal Tombs
of the First Dynasty

W.M. FLINDERS PETRIE

CAMBRIDGE
UNIVERSITY PRESS

CAMBRIDGE
UNIVERSITY PRESS

University Printing House, Cambridge, CB2 8BS, United Kingdom

Published in the United States of America by Cambridge University Press, New York

Cambridge University Press is part of the University of Cambridge.
It furthers the University's mission by disseminating knowledge in the pursuit of
education, learning and research at the highest international levels of excellence.

www.cambridge.org
Information on this title: www.cambridge.org/9781108066136

© in this compilation Cambridge University Press 2013

This edition first published 1900
This digitally printed version 2013

ISBN 978-1-108-06613-6 Paperback

ABYDOS.   STELE OF KING MERNEIT.   1 : 8.

THE ROYAL TOMBS

OF

THE FIRST DYNASTY

1900. PART I.

BY

W. M. FLINDERS PETRIE,

Hon.D.C.L., Litt.D., LL.D., Ph.D.,

EDWARDS PROFESSOR OF EGYPTOLOGY, UNIVERSITY COLLEGE, LONDON;
MEMBER OF THE IMPERIAL GERMAN ARCHAEOLOGICAL INSTITUTE;
CORRESPONDING MEMBER SOCIETY OF ANTHROPOLOGY, BERLIN;
MEMBER OF THE SOCIETY OF NORTHERN ANTIQUARIES.

With Chapter by

F. Ll. GRIFFITH, M.A., F.S.A.

―――――――

EIGHTEENTH MEMOIR OF

THE EGYPT EXPLORATION FUND

―――――――

PUBLISHED BY ORDER OF THE COMMITTEE

―――――――

LONDON
SOLD AT
THE OFFICES OF THE EGYPT EXPLORATION FUND, 37, GREAT RUSSELL STREET, W.C.
AND AT 59, TEMPLE STREET, BOSTON, MASS., U.S.A.
AND BY KEGAN PAUL, TRENCH, TRÜBNER & CO., PATERNOSTER HOUSE, CHARING CROSS ROAD, W.C.
B. QUARITCH, 15, PICCADILLY, W.; ASHER & CO., 13, BEDFORD STREET, COVENT GARDEN, W.C.
―
1900

LONDON :

PRINTED BY GILBERT AND RIVINGTON, LIMITED,

ST. JOHN'S HOUSE, CLERKENWELL.

EGYPT EXPLORATION FUND.

CONTENTS.

LIST OF PLATES

(WITH PAGES WHERE DESCRIBED).

KINGS MENTIONED IN THIS VOLUME.

Inscriptions.

D

ZESER

NARMER

} Order unknown; probably before Mena.

1st Dyn. *Manetho.*		*Sety List.*	*Tombs.*	
1.	Menes . .	Mena	= AHA — MEN	
2.	Athothis .	Teta	ZER	
3.	Kenkenes .	Ateth	ZET	} Probable order.
4.	Uenefes . .	Ata	MERNEIT	
5.	Usafais . .	Hesepti	= DEN — SETUI	
6.	Miebis . .	Merbap	= AZAB — MERPABA	
7.	Semempses .	Semenptah	= MERSEKHA — SAMENPTAH	} Order certain.
8.	Bienekhes .	Kebh	= QA — SEN (p. 23)	

2ND DYN. { PERABSEN

KHASEKHEMUI

THE
ROYAL TOMBS OF THE Ist DYNASTY.

INTRODUCTION.

1. The work described in this volume is but a portion of that carried out during the past winter, 1899-1900. In most places it is essential to finish the work in one season, and therefore to include everything in one volume. But as Abydos is a subject for several years' work, there is no need to delay the issue of the most important results while the lesser but more tedious matters are being prepared. Hence this volume does not profess to be complete, but is only some advance sheets of a longer publication which will be completed next year. Large quantities of the more bulky materials, such as jar sealings and pottery, have been left undrawn, to await issue in future; and the whole of the results of the periods of the XVIIIth Dynasty and onward will appear in a later volume. The present plates are but a portion of the material from the Ist Dynasty, with a brief account of the subjects, but so important a portion that we do not wish to keep it back for a year or two, or even a month. This has led to reversing the order, and issuing it before last year's results from Diospolis Parva, but the relative importance of the two is sufficient reason for this course.

The materials here published were prepared in Egypt during the excavating season, and some two hundred photographs and the draw-ings for over forty plates were brought home ready to use. My wife drew the tomb plans and all the marks on pottery, and I have to thank Miss Orme for inking the drawings of jar sealings. Thus I have been able to put every-thing in the printers' hands within eighteen weeks from the beginning of the excavations. I need not refer to our party at Abydos in detail, as, excepting a little occasional help, the work on the royal tombs, and the photographing and drawing, was my own share of the season's work. Mr. MacIver worked on the prehistoric age and a temple of the XIIth Dynasty; Mr. Mace on the cemetery of the XVIIIth to XXVth Dynasty; I worked some cemetery of the prehistoric and of the XXXth Dynasty; and for the Egyptian Research Account Mr. Garstang worked a cemetery of the XIIth and XVIIIth Dynasties. All this material, of much interest historically, will be published after it has been properly worked up. Some of the photographs need apology; my plates were soon exhausted by the great number of objects, a further batch from England did not arrive, and I had to fall back on very unsatisfactory plates, which were the best to be got in Cairo. Messrs. Waterlow's phototypes are better than I could have expected from such negatives.

2. It might have seemed a fruitless and

thankless task to work at Abydos after it had been ransacked by Mariette, and been for the last four years in the hands of the Mission Amélineau. It might seem a superfluous and invidious labour to follow such prolonged work. My only reason was that the extreme importance of results from there led to a wish to ascertain everything possible about the early royal tombs after they were done with by others, and to search for even fragments of the pottery. To work at Abydos had been my aim for years past; but it was only after it was abandoned by the Mission Amélineau that at last, on my fourth application for it, I was permitted to rescue for historical study the results that are here shown.

Nothing is more disheartening than being obliged to gather results out of the fraction left behind by past plunderers. In these royal tombs there had been not only the plundering of the precious metals and the larger valuables by the wreckers of early ages; there was after that the systematic destruction of monuments by the vile fanaticism of the Copts, which crushed everything beautiful and everything noble that mere greed had spared; and worst of all, for history, came the active search in the last four years for everything that could have a value in the eyes of purchasers, or be sold for profit regardless of its source; a search in which whatever was not removed was deliberately and avowedly destroyed in order to enhance the intended profits of European speculators; a search after which M. Amélineau wrote of this necropolis: "tous les fellahs savent qu'elle est épuisée." The results in this present volume are therefore only the remains which have escaped the lust of gold, the fury of fanaticism, and the greed of speculators, in this ransacked spot. These sixty-eight plates are my justification for a fourth clearance of the royal tombs of Abydos.

PUBLICATIONS REFERRING TO THE ROYAL TOMBS.

J. DE MORGAN.	*Recherches sur les Origines de l'Egypte*, ii., 1897. (*Account by G. Jéquier.*)
E. AMÉLINEAU.	*Les nouvelles Fouilles d'Abydos. Compte rendu*, 1895-6.
,,	,, ,, ,, 1896-7.
,,	,, ,, ,, 1897-8.
,,	,, ,, *in extenso*, 1896-7.
,,	*Le Tombeau d'Osiris* (*monographie*), 1899.
G. MASPERO.	Reviews in *Revue Critique* (Jan. 4, 1897; Dec. 15, 1897).
K. SETHE.	*Aeltesten geschichtlichen Denkmaeler*, in *Zeitschrift f. A. S.*, xxxv. 1.
W. SPIEGELBERG.	*Ein neues Denkmal*, in *Zeitschrift f. A. S.*, xxxv. 7.
A. ERMAN.	*Bemerkung*, in *Zeitschrift f. A. S.*, xxxv. 11.

CHAPTER I.

THE SITE OF THE ROYAL TOMBS.

3. Abydos is by its situation one of the remarkable sites of Egypt. At few places does the cultivation come so near to the edge of the mountain plateau; the great headland of Assiut, the cliffs of Thebes, or the crags of Assuan, rival it, but elsewhere there lie generally several miles of low desert between the green and the mountain. At Abydos the cliffs, about 800 feet high, come forward and form a bay about four miles across, which is nowhere more than a couple of miles deep from the cultivation (see pl. iii.). Along the edge of this bay stand the temples and the cemeteries of Abydos; while back in the circle of the hills lies the great cemetery of the founders of Egyptian history, the kings of the Ist Dynasty.

The site selected for the royal tombs was on a low spur from the hills, slightly raised above the plain, and with a deep drainage ravine on the west of it, so that it never could be flooded. Strictly speaking, the river valley, the hill line, and the tomb orientation, are all diagonal to the compass, the sides of the tombs being N.E., S.E., S.W., and N.W. But for facility of description it is assumed here that the river runs north and south, as it usually does in Egypt, and that the tombs lie correspondingly. That the ancient Egyptians recognized the diagonal direction is seen by the corner of the wood-paving of Mersekha being marked "north." In all these descriptions "north" means more exactly 44° W. of N. magnetic.

From the ruins of the Osiris temple by the cultivation, if we stand on the corner commonly called the *Kom es-Sultan*, we have before us the scene shown in pl. i. 1. The broken fore-ground stretching back for half a mile is part of the historical cemetery of Abydos. The dark walls on the right are those of the fort of the Old Kingdom age, known as the Shunet ez-Zebib. And far in the distance near the mouth of the valley is a low dark rise on the desert, formed by heaps of broken pottery around the royal cemetery. The centre of this photograph is marked on the map, pl. iii., as Φ 1.

Advancing up to the old fort our next view (pl. i. 2) is taken at the side of the little signal heap seen on the further corner of the fort in view 1; marked Φ 2 in the plan. From that we still have a stretch of the historic cemetery before us. But the distant royal cemetery is clearer, below the mouth of the valley; and the mounds are seen to be one long uniform mass, with a short ridge nearer and a little to the left. The long mass covers the royal cemetery; and the heap to the left is the rise marked as Heqreshu on the plan (pl. iii.). This rise is so called as the ushabtis of a noble of the XVIIIth Dynasty, named Heqreshu, were found here. This ground was a favourite place for high people of that age to have their ushabtis buried in, so as to be near Osiris, and ready to work in his kingdom. No human burials were found; but ushabtis of some half dozen persons were found here, and about the same number were found by the Mission Amélineau.

We next, in the view (pl. ii. 3), have gone forward to this hillock of Heqreshu, to the point Φ 3 in the plan. The foreground is strewn with broken pottery, of offerings made there in the XVIIIth Dynasty and onward. The mounds over the royal tombs now separate into the heaps of Mersekha on the left, the great banks of pottery of the Osiris shrine in the middle, and the heaps over Perabsen on the right.

Lastly, advancing a short way further, we reach the first of the great mounds of pottery offerings (marked Φ 4 on plan), and stand on it, as in fig. 4, looking on to the side of the great tomb of King Zer, which was later adopted for a cenotaph of Osiris. Such is the approach to this strange site, which, from the vast quantities of pottery here, has been called by the Arabs *Um el-Qa'ab*, "the mother of pots."

The situation is wild and silent; close round it the hills rise high on two sides, a ravine running up into the plateau from the corner where the lines meet. Far away, and below us, stretches the long green valley of the Nile, beyond which for dozens of miles the eastern cliffs recede far into the dim distance.

4.   Looking at the group of tombs, as shown on pl. iii. and pl. lix., it is seen that they lie closely together. Each royal tomb is a large square pit, lined with brickwork. Close around it, on its own level, or higher up, are small chambers in rows, in which were buried the domestics of the king. Each reign adopted some variety in the mode of burial, but they all follow the type of the prehistoric burials, more or less developed. The plain square pit, like those in which the predynastic people were buried, is here the essential of the tomb. It is surrounded in the earlier examples of Zer or Zet by small chambers opening from it. By Merneit these chambers were built separately around it. By Den an entrance passage was added, and by Qa the entrance was turned to the north. At this stage we are left within reach of the early passage-mastabas and pyramids. Substituting a stone lining and roof for bricks and wood, and placing the small tombs of domestics further away, we reach the type of the mastaba-pyramid of Seneferu, and so lead on to the pyramid series of the Old Kingdom.

The plan pl. lix. is left intentionally in out-line as the survey is not completed, and until we have accurate plans of the tombs that I have not yet opened, it is impossible to finish it uniformly. It might be supposed that the plans already published would suffice, and that I might incorporate those. But the uncertainties which surround them are so great that it is impossible to rely on them. M. Jéquier, in the *Recherches sur les Origines de l'Egypte*, ii., on p. 232 has given a plan called the "tombeau du roi *Ka*," but the form is that of the central chamber of Mersekha, and the scale shows it to be 328 inches long, while that of Qa is 428, and that of Mersekha 523 inches; its proportion of length to breadth is as 1 : 2·28, that of Qa is 1 : 1·90, and that of Mersekha 1 : 1·80; it has no entrance, and both Qa and Mersekha have wide doorways. Thus neither in size, proportion, nor detail can it be followed. Turning to the next plan, on p. 233, called "tombeau du roi *Den*," the length by the scale is 277 inches, whereas the tomb is really about 652 inches; the other details I cannot check until I clear it. The next plan, "tombeau du roi *Dja*," or Zet, is apparently intended for it, but the chambers differ from the truth in number, size, and form; the size by the scale is 355 × 429 inches, really 369 × 470 inches: and I have not yet found any trace of the passage around the tomb, which seems to be an entire misconception. The next plan, that of the "tombeau du roi *Ti*" (p. 242)—or as he should be called, Khasekhemui—is by scale 2068 inches long, by measure of the breadth 2840 long, and is stated in the text to be 83 metres or 3260 inches long: probably the text is corrupt and should read 53. The details of the tomb I cannot verify until it is cleared. Turning now to M. Amélineau's plans ("Nouvelles Fouilles, 1897-8"), the "tombeau d'Osiris," that is of King Zer,[1] is

---

[1] For this reading *Zer* (the bundle of reeds) I am indebted to Mr. Quibell's study of the sealings from here. M. Amélineau reads this sign, however, as *khent* (the group of vases), and always calls this tomb that of Osiris.

shown (p. 39) with the shortest dimension N. to
S., in the text the shortest is E. to W.; the
detail I have not yet verified. In the plan
of the tomb of Perabsen, north and south are
interchanged, and the scale is about 1 : 170 or
180, instead of 1 : 200 stated; the contraction
to the N. end is unnoticed, but details I have
not yet verified. It will thus be seen that there
was room for some fresh plans to be made of
these tombs.

5. The sequence of the tombs is to be carefully studied. As will be seen on pls. xi. 14,
xv. 16, the king whose *ka* name is *Den* is also
known as the *suten biti Setui*, a name which
Dr. Sethe has correctly suggested to be that
misfigured in the table of Abydos as Hesepti,
the fifth of the Dynasty. Further, by the
sealings shown on pl. xxvi., No. 57, the king
with *ka* name Azab is also known as Merpaba,
doubtless King Merbap, the sixth of the
Dynasty. Further, by the sealing on pl.
xxviii., No. 72, the king with the *ka* name
Mersekha is the seventh of the Dynasty, figured
in the Abydos table much like a statue of Ptah,
and called Semempses by Manetho. That this
is to be read Sem-en-ptah is very doubtful in
view of the original form of the figure, which
is best seen on the tablet pl. xvii., No. 26; it
seems more likely to be a follower, *shemsu*, or
possibly a " priest of Ptah."

Beside the absolute identification of three of
the kings with those in the list of Abydos, we
can add several proofs of relative order from
the inscriptions on vases found appropriated by
later kings. In this way a vase of Narmer (pl.
iv., No. 2) is found in the tomb of Zet, and
another erased in the tomb of Den. A vase of
Den-Setui (pl. v., No. 11) is found re-engraved
by Azab. Many vases of Azab are found
erased and re-used by Mersekha, pl. vi., Nos
9-11.

Therefore we may, from the evidence of the
tomb inscriptions alone, restore the order of the
kings as :—

Narmer
Zet

———

Den   = Setui
Azab   = Merpaba
Mersekha = Semempses.

———

Hence the order of Manetho is confirmed for
the three kings who are identified.

We may now turn to the plan, as we can be
certain that the order of building is Den, Azab,
Mersekha. It needs little notice to see that
Qa naturally follows this group. Of the earlier
tombs it seems probable that Merneit is before
Den, Zet earlier still, and Zer (or Khent) before
all these; the gradual pushing back of the tomb
sites being pretty clear. We therefore must
look on the most eastern tombs as the earliest,
and this is confirmed by private tombs to the
east of Zer, which contain a jar sealing and a
shell bracelet of King Aha. That Aha must
come very early in the Ist Dynasty is already
clear; the style of his work is certainly ruder
than anything else in the Dynasty, and the
form of the hawk on his vases is closely like
that of Narmer, who comes before Zet and Den.
Thus Aha must, from evidence of style, and
position of his objects, come within a reign of
Mena; and there is no reason for not accepting
the identification of him with Mena; especially
now that it is shown to be usual for the king's
name to be simply written below the vulture
and uraeus group.

Thus we are led to the following order of
kings :—

By tombs.	Table of Abydos.	Manetho.
Aha	Mena . . .	Menes
Zer	Teta . . .	Athothis
Zet	Atet . . .	Kenkenes
Merneit . . .	Ata . . .	Uenenfes
Den—Setui . .	Hesepti . .	Usafais
Azab—Merpaba	Merbap . .	Miebis
Mersekha . .	... ptah ?	Semempses
Qa—Sen . .	Qebh . . .	Bienekhes

and we have left yet unplaced King Narmer, who must be before Zet; King Zeser (pl. iv., No. 3), and King D (pl. xxxii., No. 32); these two last seem connected by the title being only two *neb* signs, without the vulture and uraeus. Zeser is before Den, as the piece was found re-used in Den's tomb. King D I found on a piece of vase in the Cairo Museum, where it had lain unobserved. If Narmer came after Mena there would be a difficulty, as there would be four names between Aha and Den, and only three between Mena and Hesepti; but there is no proof but what Narmer may be before Mena, as Zeser and D may be. The position of a king who seems to be named Ket ⌣ 𓅱 (pl. xi., No. 12; pl. xvii., No. 28) is also uncertain; the piece was found by the offering-place of Qa.

Thus though the Dynasty is nearly all restored in order, entirely owing to the work of this year, yet there are several puzzles still remaining for future work to solve. And the relation of the tombs of Perabsen and Khasekhemui to the others is quite untouched.

6. We may now notice the appearance and history of the royal cemetery in later times. The tombs as they were left by the kings seem to have been but slightly heaped up. The roofs of the great tombs were about six or eight feet below the surface, an amount of sand which would be easily carried by the massive beams that were used. The lesser tombs had about five feet of sand over them. But there does not seem to have been any piling up of a mound; not only is there no such excess of material remaining, but the condition of the steles, as we shall next describe, shows that the level of the soil remained uniform for a long time, whereas a mound would have been continually degrading and accumulating blown sand.

On the flat, or almost flat, ground of the cemetery the graves were marked by stone steles set upright in the open air. The great stele of Merneit (frontispiece) shows clearly the level to which it was buried; below that point the stone is quite fresh, above that the exfoliations are due to moisture soaked up from the earth, and the upper part is sand-worn. Other small steles show very plainly the lower part absolutely fresh and unaltered, and the upper part deeply sand-worn; the division between the two being within a quarter of an inch.

Each royal grave seems to have had two great steles. I found two of Merneit, one almost perished; there were two of Qa, one found by the Mission Amélineau, one by myself; and though only one has been found of Zet and Mersekha, yet one such might well be lost, as none have survived of Zer, Den, or Azab. The steles seem to have been placed on the east side of the tombs, and on the ground level. Those of Merneit had fallen into the tomb on the east side, the fragments of steles of Mersekha lay on the east side, the stele of Qa lay on the ground level at the east side, and close by it were many stone bowls, one inscribed for "the priest of the temple of Qa."

Hence we must figure to ourselves two great steles standing up, side by side, on the east of the tomb: and this is exactly in accord with the next period that we know, in which, at Medum, Seneferu had two great steles and an altar between them on the east of his tomb; and Rahotep had two great steles, one on either side of the offering-niche east of his tomb. Probably the pair of obelisks of the tomb of Antef V. at Thebes were a later form of this system. Around the royal tomb stood the little private steles of the domestics (pls. xxxi.—xxxvi.) placed in rows, thus forming an enclosure about the king.

7. The royal cemetery seems to have gradually fallen into decay; the steles were blown over or upset wantonly, and the whole site was neglected and forgotten in the later ages. There are no offering vases there of the pyramid age, nor of the Middle Kingdom. But the revived grandeurs of the XVIIIth Dynasty awakened

some interest in the tracing of the history. Tahutmes III. had a roll of ancestors compiled, which though very erratic, yet showed an interest in the past; and Sety I. succeeded in having a fairly correct list made, in which a few blunders occurred in the early names, as we see by the differences between the inscriptions of the Ist Dynasty and the Table of Abydos, but which seems to have been historically in order. This revived the interest in the cemetery which tradition had known as that of the early kings. Offerings began to be made to the kings at their tombs; but very blindly, as several places which did not contain any royal tomb were heaped up with potsherds, while some of the royal tombs (as Merneit and Azab) had scarcely anything placed on them. In this uncertainty the rise marked " Heqreshu," pl. iii., was evidently supposed to be important, though there was nothing older there than a Vth or VIth Dynasty tomb of an official named Emzaza.

A great impetus to offerings was given by the adoption of one of the royal tombs, that of king Zer, as a cenotaph of Osiris. The granite bier of Osiris placed in it was probably of the XXVIth or a later Dynasty; but in the XVIIIth Dynasty the site had been adopted as the focus of Osiris worship, the earliest of the pottery heaped over it being the blue painted jars which came in under Amenhotep II. or III. The later offerings were mainly of the XXIInd to XXVth Dynasty, during which an enormous pile of broken jars accumulated over the tomb.

In the XXVIth Dynasty a chapel was built here by Haabra, of which part of a door-jamb was found thrown into the tomb of Merneit (pl. xxxviii.); scattered like the fragments of the bier of Osiris, which we found, one by Azab and the other a furlong away on the south. Further building was done here by the Prince Pefzaauneit under Aahmes; but the interest in the site faded under the Persians, and beyond a few stray scraps of Roman pottery and glass there is nothing later found here.

At what time the burning of the woodwork took place is not fixed. It was certainly long after the original burial, as the wooden floors mostly remain quite uncharred, and the walls seldom show any burning toward the bottom. The only tombs with burnt floor are that of Merneit and part of Mersekha. In the tomb of Azab it is clear that the roof had let in sand at the south end until the chamber was nearly full, and only the corners of the upper part were exposed to the burning of the roof. Probably, therefore, the burning was due to accident. The tombs were deserted, the roofs broken in, the chambers almost full of sand. Runaway slaves and vagabonds taking refuge here would light fires and use the wood, and thus by accident the great beams would catch fire and be destroyed. Such seems to have been the source of the burning here; certainly it had nothing to do with the funeral, as scarcely any of the objects of wood, ivory, or stone, show any traces of it.

CHAPTER II.

DESCRIPTION OF THE TOMBS.

8. THE TOMB OF ZET, pl. lxi. This tomb consists of a large chamber twenty feet wide and thirty feet long, with smaller chambers around it at its level, the whole bounded by a thick brick wall, which rises seven and a half feet to the roof, and then three and a half feet more to the top of the retaining wall. The exact dimensions of these tombs are all given together in sect. 16. Outside of this on the north is a line of small tombs about five feet deep, and on the south a triple line of tombs of the same depth. And apparently of the same system and same age is the mass of tombs marked as "Cemetery W," which are parallel to the tomb of Zet. Later there appears to have been built the long line of tombs which are marked partly Z, partly W, placed askew in order not to interfere with those which have been mentioned. And then this skew line gave the direction to the next tomb, that of Merneit, and later on that of Azab. Such seems to have been the order of construction; but as the great mounds of rubbish, which I have not yet moved, stand close to the east of Zet and Cemetery W, there may be other features beneath them which will further explain the arrangement.

The private graves around the royal tomb are all built of mud brick, with a coat of mud plaster over it, and the floor is of sand, usually also coated with mud. The steles found in the graves around Zet are shown in pls. xxxiii., xxxiv., and the copies pl. xxxi., Nos. 1-16. The places of such as could be at all identified with the graves, are shown on pl. lxi. by the name from each being written on the chamber plan. Beside these steles there were often the names inscribed in red paint on the walls; these names are drawn in pl. lxiii., and are written close to the south walls of the plans. These painted names are always on the south wall of the chamber, close to the top of it. A patch of whitewash about eight or ten inches square was roughly brushed on the mud plaster of the wall; on that the hieroglyphs were painted with a broad brush. Some lines are pink, owing to the whitewash working up with the red in the brush. On a few are traces of black also. The form of inscription is much simpler than that of the steles; the *ka akh*, "glorified ka," only once appears, and there are no titles or offices, only the name. The *ka* arms often appear; but whether this refers to the *ka* of Du, A, Si, &c., or is really a compound name, Ka-du, A-kat, Si-ka, is not clear. Probably the latter is true, as the feminine *t* is added to the *ka* in two cases, which points to its being in a name. Many of these names were illegible, only fragments of the plaster remaining. Three I succeeded in removing. The few contents of these graves, left behind accidentally by previous diggers, will be fully catalogued in the next volume; a few jars and beads, and two or three pieces of inscribed stone bowls (each marked with their source in pls. iv., vi.), are all that we found.

9. TOMB OF ZET, INTERIOR, pls. lxi., lxii., lxiii. The first question about these great tombs is how they were covered over. Some have said that such spaces could not be roofed,

and at first sight it would seem almost impossible. But the actual beams found yet remaining in the tombs are as long as the widths of the tombs, and therefore timber of such sizes could be procured. In the tomb of Qa the holes for the beams yet remain in the walls, and even the cast of the end of a beam. And in the tombs of Merneit, Azab, and Mersekha are posts and pilasters to help in supporting a roof. We must therefore see how far such a roof would be practicable. The clear span of the chamber of Zet is 240 inches, or 220 if the beams were carried on a wooden lining, as seems likely. Taking, however, 240 inches length, and a depth and breadth of 10½ inches like the breadths of the floor beams, such a beam of a conifer, supported at both ends and uniformly loaded, would carry about 51,000 lbs., or 2900 lbs. on each foot of roof area. This is equal to 33 feet depth of dry sand. Hence, even if the great beams were spaced apart with three times their breadth between each, they would carry eight feet depth of sand on them; but as the height of the retaining wall is 3½ feet, the strain would be only half of the full load. It is therefore quite practicable to roof over these great chambers up to spans of twenty feet. The wood of such lengths was actually used, and if spaced out over only a quarter of the area, the beams would carry their load with full safety. Any boarding, mats, straw, &c., laid over the beams would not increase the load, as they would be lighter than the same bulk of sand. That there was a mass of sand laid over the tomb is strongly shown by the retaining wall (see pl. lxii.) around the top. This wall is roughly built, not intended to be a visible feature. The outside is daubed with mud plaster, and has a considerable slope; the inside is left quite rough, with bricks in and out (see photographs on pl. lxiv., Nos. 1, 2, 3). Such a construction shows that it was backed against loose material inside it. The top of it is finished off with a rough rounding. At the S.W.

corner this retaining wall ceases, and it seems as if this were left thus in order to gain access to the tomb for the funeral. The full thickness of the tomb wall stretches out several feet beyond even the outside of the upper retaining wall.

Turning now to the floor, the section is given in pl. lxii., and the view of it in photographs pl. lxiv., nos. 3, 4. The basis of it is mud plastering, which was whitewashed. On that were laid beams around the sides, and one down the middle: these beams were between 9 and 10·8 inches wide, and 7 to 7½ inches deep. They were placed before the mud floor was hard, and have sunk about ¼ inch into it. On the beams a ledge was recessed 6·5 to 7·7 wide, and 4·7 to 6·0 deep. On this ledge the edges of the flooring planks rested, 2 to 2·4 thick. Such planks would not bend ¼ inch in the middle by a man standing on them, and therefore made a sound floor. Over the planks was laid a coat of mud plaster ·5 to ·7 inch thick. This construction doubtless shows what was the mode of flooring the palaces and large houses of the early Egyptians, in order to keep off the damp of the ground in the Nile valley. For common houses a basis of pottery jars turned mouth down was used for the same purpose, as I found at Koptos.

The sides of the great central chamber are not clear in arrangement. The brick cross walls which subdivide them into separate cells have no finished faces on their ends. All the wall faces are plastered and whitewashed; but the ends of the cross walls are rough bricks, all irregularly in and out. Moreover, the bricks project forward irregularly over the beam line, as outlined in the plan, pl. lxii. This projection is 4 inches on the north, 4 on the east, and 2½ on the south; and on the east, one of the overhanging bricks had mud on the end of it, with a cast of upright timber on it. It seems then that there was an upright timber lining to the chamber, against which the cross walls were

built, the walls thus having rough ends projecting over the beams. The footing of this upright
plank lining is indicated by a groove left along
the western floor beam, 3·7 wide between the
ledge on the beam and the side of the flooring
planks (see plan pl. lxii.). Thus we reach the
view of a wooden chamber, lined with upright
planks 3½ inches thick, which stood 3 to 4
inches out from the wall, or from the backs
of the beams. How the side chambers were
entered is not shown; whether there was a
door to each or no. But as they were intended
to be for ever closed, and as the chambers in
two corners were shut off by brickwork all
round, it seems likely that all the side chambers
were equally closed. And thus, after the slain
domestics (p. 14) and offerings were deposited
in them, and the king in the centre hall, the roof
would be permanently placed over the whole.

The height of the chamber is proved by the
cast of straw which formed part of the roofing,
and which comes at the top of the course of
headers on edge which copes the wall all round
the chamber. Over this straw there was laid
one course of bricks a little recessed, and beyond
that is the wide ledge all round before reaching
the retaining wall. The height up to the top of
this course of headers is 89·6 in N.W. chamber,
= 90·6 in main chamber, as the floor is 1 inch
higher; 93·2 in second chamber N., = 94·2
in main; 90·0 in third chamber S., = 91·0 in
main; and 95·3 on mid W. So it varies from
90·6 to 95·3 over the main mud floor. This
implies about 92, less 4 for flooring, less probably
12 for roofing, or clear 76 inches height in the
chamber. The retaining wall is 38 inches high
inside, and 47 high outside.

Having thus cleared up the central chamber,
we should notice those at the sides. The cross
walls were built after the main brick outside
was finished and plastered. The deep recesses
coloured red, on the north side (see pl. lxiii.),
were built in the construction; where the top
is preserved entire, as in a side chamber on the

north, it is seen that the roofing of the recess
was upheld by building in a board about an
inch thick. The shallow recesses along the
south side were merely made in the plastering,
and even in the secondary plastering after the
cross walls were built. All of these recesses,
except that at the S.W., were coloured pink-
red, due to mixing burnt ochre with the white.
In the outlines of pl. lxiii. the condition of the
walls does not profess to be exactly as at
present, but more or less broken down, so
as to show the plan and detail more clearly.
The purport of these recesses is quite unknown;
but they can hardly be separated from the
red recesses on the walls of the central halls
of houses at Tell el Amarna, of the XVIIIth
Dynasty. There was also a red recess, with a
scene of worship of the tree goddess painted
over it, in a gallery of the Ramesseum. It
seemed from that as if these red recesses were
false doorways for the worship of domestic
spirits. Possibly this may be connected with
the red recesses of this tomb. The supposition
that these recesses were to hold steles is impossible, in view of the sizes of the steles, and
the finishing and colouring of the recesses.

10. THE TOMB OF MERNEIT, pls. lxi., lxiv.,
lxv. This tomb was not at first suspected, as
it had no accumulation of pottery over it; and
the whole ground had been pitted all over
by the Mission Amélineau making "quelques
sondages," without revealing the chambers or
the plan. As soon, however, as we began to
systematically clear the ground the scheme of a
large central chamber with eight long chambers
for offerings around it, and a line of private
tombs enclosing it, stood apparent. The central
chamber is very accurately built, with vertical
sides parallel to less than an inch. It is about
21 feet wide and 30 feet long, or practically
the same as the chamber of Zet (exactly
250 × 354 inches to the brick walls, the plaster
varying from ¼ to 1 inch). Around the chamber
are walls 48 to 52 inches thick, and beyond

them a girdle of long narrow chambers, 48 wide and 160 to 215 inches long. These chambers are about 6½ feet deep, but the central chamber is nearly 9 feet. Of these chambers for offerings Nos. 1, 2, 5, 7 still contained pottery in place, and No. 3 contained many jar scalings. The great stele of Merneit (frontispiece) was found lying near the east side of the central chamber; and near it was the back of a similar stele (see photograph, pl. lxiv., No. 6), on which the bottom of the *neit* and *r* signs remained, and from which a piece of the top with the top of the *neit* on it was found lying over chamber 5.

At a few yards distance from the chambers full of offerings is a line of private graves almost surrounding the royal tomb. This line is interrupted at the S. end of the W. side, similar to the interruption of the retaining wall of the tomb of Zet at that quarter. It seems therefore that the funeral approached it from that direction. In the small graves there are no red inscriptions, as in those belonging to Zet; but steles were found, the names of two of which are entered on the plan, and the figures are given in pls. xxxi., xxxiv. 17-19. A feature which could not well be shown in the plan is the ledge which runs along the side of these tombs. The black wall here figured is the width of the level edge of the pit, but beyond this a slight edging of brick rises a few inches higher.

11. THE TOMB OF MERNEIT, INTERIOR, pls. lxiv., lxv. The chamber shows signs of burning, on both the walls and the floor. A small piece of wood yet remaining on the floor indicates that it also had a wooden floor, like the other tombs. Against the walls stand pilasters of brick (see plan lxi., photograph lxiv., No. 5); and though these are not at present more than a quarter of the whole height of the wall, they originally reached to the top, as is shown by the smoking of the wall on each side, even visible in the photograph. These pilasters are entirely additions to the first building; they

stand against the plastering, and upon a loose layer of sand and pebbles about 4 inches thick. Thus it is clear that they belong to the subsequent stage of the fitting of a roof to the chamber. Such a roof would not need to be as strong as that of Zet, as there was much less depth of sand over it; so that beams only at the pilasters would serve to carry enough boards to cover it. The pilasters, however, seem to have been altogether an afterthought, as within two of the corner ones there remain the ends of upright posts, around which the brickwork was built. The holes that are shown in the floor are apparently not connected with the construction, as they are not in the mid-line where pillars are likely. The height of the chamber is 105 inches, at both E. and S.W., up to the top of a course of headers on edge around it. At the edge of chamber 2 is the cast of plaited palm-leaf matting on the mud mortar above this level, and the bricks are set back irregularly; this shows the mode of finishing off the roof of this tomb.

12. THE TOMB OF DEN-SETUI, pl. lix. From the position of this tomb it is seen to naturally follow the building of the tombs of Zet and Merneit. It is surrounded by rows of small chambers, for offerings, and for burial of domestics; but as I have only partially examined these as yet, no plan in detail is here given. The king's tomb appears to have contained a great number of tablets of ivory and ebony, fragments of eighteen having been found by us in the rubbish thrown out by the Mission Amélineau, beside one perfect tablet stolen from that work (now in the MacGregor collection), and a piece picked up (now in Cairo Museum); thus twenty tablets are known from this tomb. The inscriptions on stone vases (pl. v.) are, however, not more frequent than in previous reigns. This tomb appears to be one of the most costly and sumptuous, with its pavement of red granite; the details of it I hope to publish after its clearance next season.

13. THE TOMB OF AZAB-MERPABA, pl. lxi. This is a plain chamber, with rather sloping sides, about twenty-two feet long and fourteen feet wide ; the well-plastered face ends at a row of headers on edge, six and a half feet from the floor, and above that the wall slopes out irregularly. The surrounding wall is nearly five feet thick. Thus was included all in one block the lesser and more irregular chamber on the north, which is of the same depth and construction, fourteen feet by nine. This lesser chamber had no remains of flooring ; it contained many large sealings of jars, and seems to have been for all the funereal provision, like the eight chambers around the tomb of Merneit. Around this tomb is a circuit of small private tombs, leaving a gap on the S.W. like that of Merneit, and an additional branch line has been added on at the north. All of these tombs are very irregularly built ; the sides are wavy in direction, and the divisions of the long trench are slightly piled up, of bricks laid lengthways, and easily overthrown. This agrees with the rough and irregular construction of the central tomb and offering chamber. The funeral of Azab seems to have been more carelessly conducted than that of any of the other kings here ; only one piece of inscribed vase was in his tomb, as against eight of his found in his successor's tomb, and many other vases of his erased by his successor. Thus his palace property seems to have been kept back for his successor's use, and not buried with Azab himself. In the chambers 58, 61, 62, 63 much ivory inlaying was found, figured in pl. xxxvii. 47—60. All the tomb contents will be fully described in a future volume.

14. THE TOMB OF AZAB, INTERIOR, pls. lxv., lxvi. The entrance to the tomb was by a stairway descending from the east, thus according with the system begun by the previous king, Den. Each step is about twenty inches wide and eight inches high ; and thus descending ten steps we reach the blocking of the

doorway. On these steps, just outside of the door, were dozens of small pots, loosely piled together, of the forms marked Y in pls. xlii., xliii. These must have contained offerings made after the completion of the burial. The blocking is made by planks and bricks (see lxv., lower right hand). Two grooves were left in the brickwork of the passage sides, plastered over like the passage. Across the passage stretched planks of wood about two inches thick, with ends lodging in the grooves. To retain them in place on each other another upright plank was placed against them in the groove, and jammed tight by bricks wedged in. Then the whole outside of the planking was covered by bricks loosely stacked as headers ; these can be seen in the photograph (lxvi., No. 2), the planking having decayed away from before them.

The chamber was floored with planks of wood laid flat on the sand, without any supporting beams as in other tombs. These planks are 2·0 inches thick where best preserved. They were cut to order before fitting into the tomb, and hence in several places they were slightly too long. This has been roughly remedied by chopping away the mud wall near the bottom so as to let in the ends (see lxvi. 1), or scraping down so as to jam the board down into place.

The support of the roof was by wooden posts, as in the tomb of Merneit ; but here they were not cased round or supplemented by brick piers. The base of one post remained in place at the N.E. corner (see lxv.) : it was 4×17 inches, and stood free on the floor, not let in at all, 3 inches from the N. and 1 inch from the E. sides. That this was not accidental in place is shown at the N.W. corner, where the N. wall has been much chopped away in order to let back an irregularly bent post. Beyond this there are no traces, either from attachment or from burning, of uprights or divisions, or of pilasters on the walls.

The roof must have been at about six feet over the floor, as the walls are finished up to 78 inches high, and then are rougher and more sloping above that. The plastering went on simultaneously with the building: this is shown by a course of headers on edge at 48 inches, up to which the plastering has been done at once, while above that the plastering was separate. The highest part of the wall is 89 inches high, the ground at the top step being 97 inches. The roof broke in at the middle of the south end, and let sand run in enough to fill the chamber at that end. Thus only the two corners were left exposed to the fire in the burning of the roof.

15. THE TOMB OF MERSEKHA-SEMEMPSES, pl. lx. This tomb is 44 feet long and 25 feet wide, a pit surrounded by a wall over five feet thick. The surrounding small chambers are only three to four feet deep, where perfect; while the central pit is still $11\frac{1}{2}$ feet deep, though broken away at the top.

Few of the small chambers still contained anything. Seven steles were found, the inscriptions of which are marked in the chambers of the plan : the photographs, pls. xxxv., xxxvi., show these in Nos. 29, 30, 31, 32, 35, 36, 46; and other steles on these plates were also found here, scattered so that they could not be identified with the tombs. The most interesting are two steles of dwarfs, 36, 37, which show the dwarf type clearly; with one (chamber M) were found bones of a dwarf. Another skeleton of a dwarf was in chamber L; probably the other stele had belonged to this. In a chamber on the east was a jar and a copper bowl (xii. 11); this last is the only large piece of metal-work that we found; it shows the hammer marks, and is roughly finished, with the edge turned over to leave it smooth. We here have a good example of the rude state of metal-work at that time. The ivory leg of a casket (xii. 9) was found loose in the rubbish before the door-way of the tomb, and had doubtless been part of

the royal furniture. The small compartments in the south-eastern chambers were probably intended to hold the offerings placed in the graves : the dividing walls are only about half the depth of the grave.

16. THE TOMB OF MERSEKHA, INTERIOR, pls. lx., lxvi., lxvii. The structure of the interior is at present uncertain. Only in the corner by the entrance (lxvi. 4) was the wooden flooring preserved; several beams (one now in Cairo Museum) and much broken wood was found loose in the rubbish. M. Amélineau states that the tomb was entirely burnt, and the floor carbonized, but there are few traces of fire about the walls. The floor, where it yet remains, is made like others; beams, 8 inches wide and 10 high, form the frame on which the planks of the floor rest on recessed ledges (see pl. lx., lxviii.). There has been a wider and shallower cutting also at each side of the corner, as if some skin of finer wood had been laid over it. The corner plank has two holes through it, and the sign meht, "north" cut on it. This shows that the woodwork was prepared elsewhere, and brought here ready; and this was also seen in the tomb of Azab, by the chopping of the walls to fit the wood. This piece of floor is not symmetrically placed, being 50 inches from the N. end, and so agreeing nearly to the 56 inches projection of the pilaster at the S. end (see lxvi. 3), whereas it is only 19 inches from the entrance wall. At about a third of the length from the S. end was a soft hole in the sand floor, which may be the place of a pillar. The span of 24 feet is too great to suppose it roofed with single beams across, and the pilaster at the S. end suggests that the beams were supported or divided in the middle. Hence it seems likely that the places of the main beams were about the lines dotted in the plan, pl. lx. There is no sign of holes for the beams, and no evidence as to the roofing level.

The entrance is 9 feet wide, and was blocked by loose bricks, flush with wall face, as seen in photograph lxvi. 4. Another looser walling further out, also seen in the photograph, is probably that of plunderers to hold back the sand. The section of the side wall of the entrance is given on pl. lxvii.

On clearing the entrance, the native hard sand was found to slope down to about four feet above the floor, and then to drop to floor level at about two and a half feet outside of the outer wall of the tomb. Here the space was filled to three feet deep with sand saturated with ointment. The fatty matter was that so common in the prehistoric times, in this Ist Dynasty, and onward in the XVIIIth Dynasty; hundredweights of it must have been poured out here, and the scent was so strong when cutting away this sand that it could be smelt over the whole tomb. In clearing this entrance was found the perfect ivory tablet of king Semempses (xii. 1 and xvii. 26); and his identity with the king Mersekha of this tomb was proved by the sealing No. 72, pl. xxviii.

17. THE TOMB OF KING QA, pls. lx., lxvi., lxvii. This tomb, which is the last of the Dynasty, shows a more developed stage than the others. Chambers for offerings are built on each side of the entrance passage, and this passage is turned to the north, as in the mastabas of the IIIrd Dynasty, and in the pyramids. The whole of the building is hasty and defective. The bricks were mostly used too new, probably less than a week after being made. Hence the walls have seriously collapsed in most of the lesser chambers; only the one great chamber was built of firm and well-dried bricks. In the four chambers along the passage, 16, 18, 23, 24, the walls have had to be strengthened by thickening them, so as to leave wide ledges near the top, shown by the outlines in the plan: in chamber 23 the south side had crushed forward with its weight, and so taken a slice off the chamber width. And the wall had slipped away sideways into chamber 12, and was thus left ruined. In the small chambers along the

east side the long wall between chambers 10 and 5 has crushed out at the base, and spread against the pottery in the grave 5, and against the wooden box in grave 2. Hence the objects must have been placed in those graves within a few days of the building of the wall, before the mud bricks were hard enough to carry even four feet height of wall. The burials of the domestics must therefore have taken place all at once, immediately the king's tomb was built; and hence they must have been sacrificed at the funeral.

The graves still contained several burials, and these are all figured in position on the plan; five have the head to the north, and only one to the south; all are contracted. Thus the attitude was that of the prehistoric burials, also found in the IIIrd Dynasty at Medum, and in the Vth Dynasty at Deshasheh. But the direction is that of the historic burials. Hence the customs have a greater break between the prehistoric and the Ist than between the Ist and the Vth Dynasty. The boxes in which the bodies were placed vary from 36 to 45 inches long, and 18 to 27 inches wide; the average is 38 × 22. The height is usually 16 or 17 inches, in one case only 9 inches. The boards are 1·2 inches thick. The sides appeared to have been slightly pegged together, and they were found as merely loose boards much decayed. The interior and space around the coffin were filled with perfectly clean white sand, which must have been intentionally filled in. But the coffins can hardly have been made separately to fit the bodies; in grave 8 the body is bent back-outward, naturally, but the head has been twisted round so as to bring the face to the back; perhaps it was actually cut off, as the atlas was an inch beyond the foramen. There were no personal ornaments or armlets found in any grave, though I carefully cleared every coffin myself. The pottery placed in the chambers is all figured in position in the plan; and the forms will be seen, with the references to the chambers, in pls. xl. to xliii. In the S.E corner of chamber 9 were some baskets, of which one and part of another could be removed.

Few steles were found, only three in all, but these were larger than those of the earlier graves. One is hardly legible (xxxi., xxxvi. 47), being faintly hammered on the stone face; it shows the hare *un*, and nothing else is certain. The other stele, No. 48, is the longest and most important inscription known of this age; it is carefully reproduced on pl. xxx. The general surface is hammered out, but has never been finished by graving; the full lines are the traces of the black ink drawing, and the red lines show the first sketch. The description of it is given more fully in dealing with the private steles, sect. 20. The stele of the king Qa was found lying over chamber 3; it is like that found by M. Amélineau, carved in black quartzose stone. Photographs have not yet been taken of it, so it will be reproduced in the following volume. Near it, on the south, were dozens of large pieces of fine alabaster bowls, and one of diorite with the inscription for the "Priest of the temple of King Qa" (ix. 12), showing that the shrine of offerings for Qa was probably on this side.

Among various objects found in these chambers should be noted the fine ivory carving from chamber 23, showing a bound captive (pl. xii. 12, 13; xvii. 30), described on p. 23; the large stock of painted model vases in limestone in a box in chamber 20 (pl. xxxviii. 5, 6); the set of perfect vases found in chamber 21 (xxxviii. 8); the fine piece of ribbed ivory (xxxvii. 79); a piece of thick gold foil covering of a *hotep* table, patterned as a mat, found in the long chamber west of the tomb; the deep mass of brown vegetable matter in the N.E. chamber; the large stock of corn between chambers 8 and 11; and the bed of currants, ten inches thick though dried, which underlay the pottery in chamber 11. In chamber 16 were large dome-shaped jar sealings with the name of Azab, and on one of them the ink-written signs of the "king's ka" (xxxii. 35).

The entrance passage has been closed with rough brick walling at the top. It is curiously turned askew, as if to avoid some obstacle, but the chambers of the tomb of Den do not come near its direction. After nine steps the straight passage is reached, and then a limestone portcullis slab bars the way, let into grooves on either side; it was moreover backed up by a buttress of brickwork in five steps behind it. All this shows that the rest of the passage must have been roofed in so deeply that entry from above was not the obvious course. The inner passage descends by steps, each about five inches high, partly in the slope, partly in the rise of the step. The side chambers open off this stairway by side passages a little above the level of the stairs.

18. THE TOMB OF QA, INTERIOR, pls. lx., lxvi., lxvii. The structure of this tomb is rather different from any other. Instead of the timber being an entirely separate structure apart from the brick, the brick sides seem here to have been very loosely built against the timber sides. All around the chamber were great beams 10 to 13 inches deep, and 9 inches wide, recessed to hold the ends of the flooring planks, and with deep mortice holes at intervals to hold upright posts. The beam section and place of holes is seen on pl. lxvii., and the ends of the posts still in place in the photograph, lxvi. 6. The brickwork close to the chamber sides is so loose and rough that it has nearly all fallen away, but on the west side of the doorway it remains, projecting over the beam, and evidently filling in originally up to the plank lining. This lining must have been fastened on to the upright posts, and was absolutely essential if we look to the very rough loose brickwork, which was certainly so constructed because it was hidden.

Some detail yet remains of the wooden floor,

planned on the lower part of pl. lxvii. There
were two grooves or troughs across it, and two
planks running at right angles to the others.
There seems no reason to assume that the
chamber was all one, without subdivision;
probably these grooves are the places for fittings
or panels.

The roofing is distinct in this tomb. Large
holes for the beams remain in the walls, with
red burning round each, and in one a mud cast
of the rough hewn end of the beam. These
beam holes are marked on the plan (pl. lx.), and
are not opposite to one another. This implies
that there was an axial beam, and that the side
beams only went half across the chamber. A
hole in the floor still retained part of an upright post; this was not in the true axis, but
as much to one side as the post at the side of
the doorway. Probably therefore the axial
beam ran rather to one side of the chamber, as
dotted on the plan. The greater depth of the
beam holes on the east side would imply that
about an equal length of beam was used on
either side. As this is the only tomb with the
awkward feature of an axial doorway, it is
interesting to note how the beam was placed out
of the axis to accommodate it. There is no
evidence that the axial beam was a ridge beam,
on the contrary the holes seem to show that the
side beams were horizontal. Above the side
beams is a plastered wall with a moderate
batter, probably to retain the coat of sand
over the roof, as in the tomb of Zet. The thin
white lines left in the brickwork of the plan
show the place of finished faces in the brickwork.

The interior of the chamber is 208·8 and 209
inches across between the floor beams, 410 and
412 in length between beams. This was doubtless the size of the wooden chamber, as the posts
are set back 2·0 to 2·4 from the beam face, and
that is about the usual thickness of planks in
these tombs. The height from the top of the
floor planks to the base of the beam holes, where

is a row of headers on edge, 101½ inches; the
foot of the plastered upper wall is 115½, and the
top of that wall 162 inches. So the chamber
was intended to be 10 × 20 cubits, and 5 cubits
high.

19. For convenience of reference the principal measurements of the tombs (in inches) are
here placed together.

Tomb of Zet; see sect. 9 :—
Length inside extreme   . N. 470·0 ·S. 481·5
Breadth   „   „   . E. 369·5 W. 369·0
Length   „   over beams   mid. 366·2
Breadth   „   „   . E. 241·7 W. 240·5

	Chambers.	Walls.
Along N. side, from W. . .	70·5	15·5
	50·5	15·5
	43·0	16·5
	26·0	17·0
	28·5	17·5
	31·0	15·5
	31·5	16·0
	27·5	17·0
	31·0	
Along E. side, from N. . .	68·	16·5
	56·5	16·5
	59·5	17·
	57·	16·
	62·5	
Along S. side, from E. . .	39·5	17·
	53·0	17·5
	65·5	16·9
	73·2	18·0
	21·0	14·7
	64·7	15·9
	33·4	11·2
	20·0	

Height 89·6 to 95·3.

Deducting 2 × 6·8 from the dimensions over
beams in order to find actual dimensions in
wooden chamber, we have 352·6 × 228·1 or
226·9 for the chamber; or 17 cubits of 20·74
and 11 cubits of 20·73 to 20·63.

Tomb of Merneit ; see sect. 11 :—

Inner chamber, E. and W. 354 ; N. and S. 250.

   ,, ,, high, 105.

Offering chambers, over all, W. 557 ; N. 454 ; S. 457.

 Offering chambers, lengths, 160 to 215.

 Cubit, 20·63 to 20·83 ; average, 20·75.

Tomb of Azab ; see sect. 14 :—

Length at base . . E. 258 W. 257·2

Breadth at base . . N. 165 S. 163·5

 At top these dimensions are 7½ to 20 larger.

Offering chamber :

Length at base . . N. 161 S. 161

Breadth at base . . E. 97 W. 98

 At top these dimensions are 13 to 23 larger.

 Stairway width 63 wide below to 76 above.

 By tomb chamber cubit 20·44 to 20·64, mean 20·57.

Tomb of Mersekha ; see sect. 16 :—

Length inside . . E. 656 W. 651

Breadth . . . N. 291·4 S. 293·1

    at 60 up 295·2 mid. 296·0

Along S. side E. 130·4 31·5 pil. 131·2 W.

Along E. side S. 523·0 107 door 26 N.

	Wall.	Chamber.	Wall.	Chamber.	Wall.
On N. side	59	71	10	60	
E. ,,	67	50	16	64	16
S. ,,	60	94	0	0	0
W. ,,	62	46	16	42	10

Greatest height 139, but incomplete.

Tomb of Qa ; see sect. 18 :—

Length inside of beams E. 410, W. 412·5.

Breadth inside of beams N. 208·8, S. 203, mid. 209·2.

Depth from sand 110 under beams, 124 slope to 170.

Depth from floor 101½ under beams, 115½ slope to 161½.

	Wall.	Door.	Wall.	Door.	Wall.
Along E. side passage	76	26	109	28	8

 Cubit 20·5 to 20·88, mean 20·72.

Every chamber was measured, and the details of positions of objects drawn at the time of clearing ; but it seems needless to state all the figures, as they are plotted in the plans. The above dimensions are the only ones from which any deductions are likely to be required.

The mean values of the cubit are 20·70, 20·75, 20·57, 20·72 inches. Probably 20·72 was the standard cubit of that age.

CHAPTER III.

THE OBJECTS DISCOVERED.

20. THE STONE VASES, pls. iv.—x. The enormous mass of fragments of stone vases, mainly bowls and cups, found in the tombs has not yet been fully worked over. Roughly speaking, between 10,000 and 20,000 pieces of vases of the more valuable stones were found; and a much larger quantity of slate and alabaster. The latter it was impossible to deal with, beyond selecting such pieces as showed the forms. In many cases a large group of fragments which were found together was kept apart, and sorted in hopes of finding that they would fit; but it was seldom that more than a very few could be joined. The scattering of pieces has been so thorough during the various plunderings of the ground, that pieces of the same bowl are found on the opposite sides of a tomb, or even in different tombs. To sort over and reunite the fragments of individual bowls out of 50,000 or 100,000 pieces, among stones with so little variety as slate and alabaster, and after a great part had already been carried away by previous diggers, was beyond the time and attention that our party could give. My experience in dealing with the far more promising material of the valuable stones shows how hopeless it would be to get results from the others.

The less common stones were, however, thoroughly dealt with. Every fragment was kept, the pieces from each tomb separately. Those from one tomb were then sorted into about fifteen or twenty classes of materials. Next all the pieces of one material were sorted over, placing all brims together, all middle pieces with the axis upright, and all bases together. Then every possible trial of fitting was ex-haustively gone through. In result a group of say 200 fragments of one material, from one tomb, would be mainly united into perhaps 20 or 30 lots, each the pieces of one vessel, and leaving less than half over as irreducible residue. In this way, out of the tombs of Azab, Mersekha, and Qa, I have put together parts of about 200 vases; these are in most cases about a quarter to a half of the vase, enough to draw the whole outline. These outlines remain yet to be copied. And all the fragments from Zet, Merneit, and Den have yet to be sorted.

The materials I avoid specifying at present, as many of them need careful study to define them properly. The names of materials here used on the plates are therefore intentionally vague. The frequent metamorphic limestones and breccias are here only named "meta-morphic"; the saccharine marbles with grey and green bands are named "grey marble"; the frequent opaque white, with grey veins (geobertite?) is named "white marble"; and "volcanic ash" covers everything between slate and breccia. To attempt precision before a full study of the stones would only lead to errors. We now turn to some individual notes.

21. THE INSCRIPTIONS, pls. iv.—x. Pl. iv. 1. This piece of Aha was bought from the son of M. Amélineau's reis, who had a great supply of fragments. We found a seal of Aha, and a shell bracelet with apparently Aha on it, in the ground east of Zer, so no doubt this piece came thence.

2. The piece of Narmer is part of a great alabaster cylinder; in the rubbish of Den was found a similar jar with a relief inscription

ground away, the traces of which well agree to this name. The style of the hawk is the same as on the work of Aha, and very different from that of any other king in this Dynasty, pointing to Narmer having reigned just before or after Mena.

3. This is the only piece of Zeser, and being found in an early tomb here it cannot be connected with Zeser the third king of the IIIrd Dynasty. Rather is it like a piece of bowl of an unknown king D, which I found lying at the Cairo Museum (xxxii. 32); both have the *nebti* without the vulture and uraeus, apparently an earlier form. Even Aha-Mena used the animal figures over the *nebti;* and these two names being superfluous to the Ist Dynasty, suggests that they belong, with Narmer, to the Dynasty of ten kings who are said to have reigned 350 years before Menes. Further excavation may clear this matter. The fragment of ivory of Den appears in its proper place in pl. xi.

4. This finely cut group is unfortunately imperfect; several more pieces of the bowl were found with it, but none to complete the inscription.

5. This group is the same as found scratched on pottery at the tomb of Zer, according to M. Amélineau, who reads it (Osiris, p. 43) as *ap khet* (horns and staircase).

6. This seems to be a name, *Hotep-her*, apparently repeated as *Her-hotep* on a stele published by De Morgan, No. 808; see copy, pl. xxxii.

7. This fragment was found in the tomb of Merneit, and very unluckily has just lost the name. It is deeply cut on a piece of a large crystal bowl.

8 seems to be a private name, Sunaukh.

9, 10. Fragments of brown slate, the second with three jars.

Pl. v. 1. This piece of a thin delicate bowl is the only one with the full drawing of the hieroglyph of Neit, as on the great stele (frontispiece); all the other bowls have merely crossed arrows. Beyond on the left are apparently the same signs as on No. 3.

2, 3, 4, 6, 7. All these are of burnt slate, of a bright brown. At first I supposed such slate to have been accidentally burnt in the burning of the tomb; but a bowl, found in a private grave, W 33, which had no trace of burning, showed that this brown slate had been altered naturally by an eruption. No. 2 has the *per hez*, or "white house," while 4 and 6 both name the *hat-s* as the palace name, adding *hez* above it in 7. The *khent* sign in No. 2, of vases set in a stand, should be noted. The pieces 5 were found scattered in the tomb of Mersekha; they belong to an erased inscription, and after finding the Merneit vases we can easily see the crossed arrows of Neit on the left; on the right are traces of rectangular signs. This is the only piece of Merneit identified as being re-used; there may have been others now completely erased. But it is noticeable that eight out of nine inscriptions of his are on slate. No. 3 is kept at Cairo.

8, 9, are well-cut pieces of crystal cups of Setui; the latter with an added inscription of Azab-Merpaba. There is a fine style about all the carving of Setui, both in stone and ivory, which is more dignified than that of any of the other kings.

10 is a fragment of slate found in the tomb of Setui; but the work looks rougher, and it may well belong to some earlier king.

11 is a beautiful piece of calcite with green patches. It was usurped by Azab, and is the only piece of his that we found in his tomb.

12, a fine piece of red limestone, has a boldly cut name of Setui, followed by a rougher cutting of Merpaba. The latter shows that the signs which have been read as *neter* below the hawks on the inscriptions of Khasekhemui are the usual standards, as they also appear on pl. vi. 4, and on the palette of Narmer. This piece is kept at Cairo.

Pl. vi. 1. This slate bowl was found scattered on different sides of the tomb, as were also the two pieces reunited in No. 3.

2 is a piece of a large alabaster cylinder jar, with coarse cutting.

5 are two fragments of a crystal cup with the name Merpaba, but one narrow slip between these pieces is lost.

8 is part of a very fine bowl in pink gneiss, the only example of such; it was found with two other fine bowls in the grave W 33. The inscription gives the name of the palace of Azab, *Qed-hotep*. One piece of crystal cup of Azab, not figured here, was kept at Cairo.

Many alabaster cylinder jars in the tomb of Mersekha had roughened places on them, and at first it seemed as if they were merely unfinished; but some traces of signs were found nearly erased, and this led to searching them all carefully. Every piece of alabaster and slate that was found was therefore closely looked at, usually in slanting sunlight, to find erased inscriptions. Three are shown here: on 9 the traces of the door frame and of the heart sign are seen; on 10 is part of a large hawk, and on 11 nearly the whole *ka* name is clearly seen.

Pl. vii. 1 is the only instance here of the three birds group so usual on vases of Aha. The birds of Aha look most like ostriches (see De Morgan, Nos. 558, 662), while these are more like plovers; neither would be taken for the *ba* bird of later times, and probably these are intended for *rekhyt*.

2, 3. Only two names of Mersekha were found on vases, and most of the stonework in his tomb seems to have belonged to Azab, as every piece on pl. vi. (except No. 8) came from the tomb of Mersekha. The last sign on No. 3 scarcely looks like *kha*, more resembling a fish; but the well-cut cylinder impressions (xxviii. 73, 76, 77) leave no doubt that the sign is *kha*. It is to be noted that the *s* sign always has the short side forward in this name, on these two vases, and on all the

seals on pl. xxviii., beside Nos. 17, 20, 34, and 41. This was not universal then, as the *s* is the usual way of later times on seals, 5, 6, 7, 24, 25, 30, 32, 33, 40, 49, 64, and 65; so it seems that there was no fixed rule as in later ages.

4. This fine piece of crystal cup is united from two widely scattered fragments. The lower part is a *hat* sign, as the line on the left is too near the middle to be the side of the square, and it must be the corner enclosure of the *hat*. So this reads *Neb hat ankh*. There is also a scrap of a sign above the animal, which seems to be probably a large hunting dog.

5 is a piece of a large alabaster cylinder jar, with the festival sign on it, raised on a platform which has steps at the end. This figure is best seen on viii. 7, xi. 5, and xiv. 12. On the basis are three signs (?) *SN*. On No. 7 is *N*, and on No. 8 is *SN· · · ·* All of these refer to the Sed festival.

6 is a palimpsest crystal bowl; of the earlier inscription traces remain in spite of the scraping and re-polishing of it, and the sign *su* was brought up clearly by careful wiping over with ink. The later inscription is *Sed heb*, the "Sed festival."

9 is a piece of black pottery placed here on account of its inscription. The signs *ka*, a door (?), and *mer*, are clear. The unknown sign is like one in an ink-written inscription on slate from Abydos, now at Cairo (xxxii. 33).

10 is on a coarse piece of an alabaster cylinder jar; it is the name of Azab's city or palace, *Hor-dua-kh*, as on the seal xxvi. 63.

11, 12 are two inscriptions which cannot be explained yet. The double-headed axe, after the "royal house" on 12, also appears in the hands of the warriors on a slate palette.

Pl. viii. 1 is on a piece of a large white bowl, and is better cut than any of the others of this reign. It is now in the Cairo Museum.

5 shows that it belonged to the priest of the shrine of Qa, like the bowl ix. 12.

6, 7, both refer to the Sed festival; the upper

part of 7 was not fitted on before photographing, but is given separately as 7a, and is outlined in place above 7.

9 has a boat on it somewhat like the prehistoric boats, high at both ends, and having two cabins.

11, 12, 13, 14, pl. ix. 1, 2, 3, all refer to the two buildings named Sa-ha-neb and Hor-pa-ua. No. 1, pl. ix., clears up the difference between these; at the right are parts of an inscription like that on No. 3, showing that the building Hor-pa-ua was first inscribed along with the king's name; and then later the building Sa-neb-ha was inscribed on the bowl. Thus the "house of the sole Horus"—Hor-pa-ua—was the name of the palace; and the "house of all fortune"—Sa-ha-neb—was the name of the tomb, where the bowl was later deposited. A variant is seen on the piece of a great alabaster cylinder jar " Hor-ha-sa." The details of these inscriptions are considered by Mr. Griffith in his account.

Pl. x. 1 to 7. These are some of the pieces of stone bowls inscribed with ink. 1 and 2 are very illegible, owing to being faintly marked on dark slate; but on 1 is the name of Setui, though found in the tomb of Mersekha. These will be drawn and published on their reaching England. 4 has the name of the crocodile *hems*.

22. IVORY TABLETS, pls. x. to xvii. Pl. x. 8. This slip of blackened ivory, and the triangular piece xi. 2, were both from the inlaying of a box or furniture. No. 8 is now kept at Cairo. For a drawing of xi. 2, see xiii. 1.

9 is the end of a small casket, with grooves and holes on the back for joining it to the sides. Unfortunately it was broken in finding, and the piece with the serpent was lost; but the tail of the serpent is still visible (see drawing xiii. 2), and it was found in the tomb of Zet, so there can be no doubt of its source. The last sign is like the prehistoric amulet often found. (*Naqada*, lviii. Q 709.5; lxi., 4.)

We shall here follow the order of the drawings (pls. xiii. to xvii.), as the photographs (pls. x. to xii.) are somewhat out of order owing to only part of the objects having been photographed in Egypt and the remainder in England.

xiii. 3, part of an ivory tablet of Zet (see xi. 1) found in his tomb. 3a is the back.

4, a fragment of ivory, for inlaying like 1; from tomb of Zet.

5 is part of an ivory tablet (x. 10) from a private grave Z 3. The figure of a man pounding enters into the name of the palace of Setui (xv. 16).

6 is part of an ivory boat, apparently. The position is shown by the flat base; the surface of the sides is mostly flaked away, so that the form is uncertain. On the top is a flight of steps leading up. The name of Zet is on the side, and it was found in his tomb.

7, 7a (pl. xiv.), a piece of an ivory tablet, gives a portrait of Den-Setui (see also x. 13). It shows the double crown fully developed, and the traces of colour are red for the Lower crown, white for the Upper, as later on. This piece is kept in Cairo. The *ankh* on the reverse has the divided tails as on the vase vii. 4.

8 is a fragment (see xi. 8) with Den in the attitude shown on the sealing drawn in pl. xxxii. 39. A part of a sign on the reverse is placed beside it.

9 shows Setui standing with staff and mace, preceded by standards (see also x. 14).

10 is a fragment of ivory (xi. 10) with numerals "1200," as on the ebony tablets xv. 16, 18.

11 is a piece of a thick tablet with apparently the same numerals (see xi. 6).

12 is a piece of ivory, with signs also on the back, 12a (see xi. 5). This is one more mention of the Sed festival, so often found on the stone vase inscriptions. These festivals have been discussed, as to whether they were every 30 years of a reign, or at fixed intervals of 30 years. The latter is the only use which

would agree with their undoubtedly astronomical origin, by the shift of the moveable calendar one week every 30 years, and one month every 120 years at the Great Sed festival. I have also already shown (*History*, ii. 32) how these festivals do not fall on the 30th year of the reigns, and often were in reigns of less than 30 years. Now we have this again illustrated. These festivals are named on the tablet of Setui (xiv. 12), on vases of Mersekha (vii. 5, 6, 7, 8), and on vases of Qa (viii. 6, 7), but never by Azab.

Now in Manetho the reigns of these kings are 20, 18, and 26 years, not one reaching 30 years. Moreover, we can test whether a series of 30-year intervals will fall in these reigns. Taking approximately the dates given in my History, i. 27*, we have :—

	B.C.	30-year intervals.
	4604	
Hesepti = Setui		4588-4
	4584	
Merpaba		
	4558	
Semenptah		4558-4
	4540	
Kebh = Qa.		4528-4
	4514	

So there is only a range of 4 years left possible for the 30-year cycle to fall upon within these reigns; and if Merpaba had a Sed festival, it would have upset the series. As it is—crediting Manetho's reigns—we have the Sed cycle fixed to within 4 years in the Ist Dynasty. We see then that all the evidence from these inscriptions is in favour of a fixed cycle of 30 years, quite independent of the kings' reigns. This cycle implies the loss of the day in leap years, which causes the shift of the calendar; and hence implies the calendar of 365 days being in use as early as the middle of the Ist Dynasty, and the known loss of a day in four years.

14 (pl. xv.) is a piece of a finely cut ivory tablet (see xi. 9), which shows part of the palace name, *nub hat* and the man pounding, as in No. 16.

15 is a chip of an ebony tablet, with part of the palace name, and the hawk and *sahu biti* (see xi. 3).

16 is the most important tablet, though the lower edge has not been found (see xi. 14). The scene of the king dancing before Osiris seated in his shrine is the earliest example of a ceremony which is shown on the monuments down to Roman times; he bears the *hap* and a short stick instead of the oar; the three semicircles on each side are, even at this early stage, unintelligible. The inscriptions below, referring to the festival, will be dealt with by Mr. Griffith; but we should note that the royal name Setui occurs in the lower register, so this tablet is good evidence for that king being Den, besides the clay sealings not yet published. Beyond there is the name of Den, and that of the royal seal-bearer Hemaka, which occurs so often on the jar sealings. The palace name is written with *nub*, apparently a hatchet, and the man pounding, for which see Nos. 5 and 14. The two signs after *suten* look like different forms of hatchet, see also Nos. 15, 26, 29. For the numerals " 1200 " at the bottom edge compare also Nos. 10, 11, 18. This tablet was crusted with melted resin, harder than the wood; and the only way to clean it was by powdering the resin with a needle, while watching it with a magnifier : so it is possible that some point may not have been fully cleaned out.

17 is a piece of another ebony tablet, a duplicate of the previous one (see xi. 15); but it is useful as showing a different grouping of the signs, which helps the explanation of them.

18 is another ebony piece, somewhat like the previous pieces (see xi. 4) ; but it shows a place name beginning Unt . . . , and also the royal name of King Setui.

Pl. xvi. 19. A piece of a very thick ivory tablet, much burnt : see xi. 16.

20. Part of a well-cut ivory tablet, finely polished, blackened with burning: see x. 11. The inscription seems to refer to the great chiefs coming to the tomb of Setui; and the figure of the tomb is the oldest architectural drawing known. It appears to show the tomb chamber at the left, with a slight mound over it. The tall upright may perhaps show the steles at the tomb, standing up like the poles in front of the shrine at Medum (*Medum*, ix.); see also poles at the side of a shrine of Tahutmes II. (L., *D.*, iii. 15). Next is apparently a slope descending to the tomb, the stairway of the tomb; while at the right is a diagram of the cemetery of graves in rows around the tomb, with the small steles standing up over the graves. The square enclosure of the graves, as in pl. lxi., each with a small stele over it, must have been a marked feature in the appearance of this cemetery.

21—24. Fragments photographed, 21 in xi. 11; 23 in xi. 7; 24 in xi. 17.

25. Two pieces of apparently the same tablet, judging by thickness, work, and colour.

Another piece of Setui is shown in x. 12, but not drawn. It is the edge of a thick piece from some furniture.

Pl. xvii. 26. This ivory tablet of Mersekha was found in the doorway of his tomb: see xii. 1. It is deeply cut, and coloured with red and black as shown in the drawing. The formula is much like that on the Palermo Stone, and without going into the interpretation of it we may note the remarkable reading of Horus as Heru, written with three hawks, like Khnumu written with three rams (*Season in Egypt*, xii., 312); the figure of Tahuti seated accords with the early worship of the baboon, for which see the diorite baboons in the granite Temple of Khafra. The figure which is placed for the king's name is like that on the sealing (xxviii. 72), but differs from the figure of Ptah in the Table of Abydos. This figure can hardly be intended for Ptah; and it seems as if it might be a *shemsu*, and so give the Greek form

Semempses, or else a *sam* priest of Ptah. The group of *suten* and two axes occurs also on the Setui tablet, xi. 14. And the name Henuka is seen on the tablet No. 28.

27. This fragment of royal titles was found in the tomb of Mersekha: see xi. 18.

28. This half tablet of ivory was found by the offering place of Qa, on the east of the tomb. The *ka* name appears to end with the arm, and hence it might be supposed to be of Qa; but the signs after the *suten biti* cannot be so read, and look much more like *ket*, with the small bird determinative: see xi. 12.

29. Part of a thin ivory tablet, see xii. 2: found on the east of the tomb of Qa. It seems to give an unknown royal name Sen . . . below the vulture and uraeus. As Qa succeeded Mersekha, we should expect to find the name of Kebh. It seems possible that a *sen* sign with very tall base (as on a stele, pl. xxxiv. 13) was mistaken by a later scribe for the vase *kebh*, and the *n* below for a determinative of water. After seeing Setui made into Hesepti, Merpaba into Merbap, and the figure on xvii. 26 turned into a statue of Ptah, we can well believe in a possible confusion of the early form of *sen* and *kebh*.

30. This ivory carving is the most important artistic piece that was found. It is carved on the back with the knots and bracts of a reed, and imitates one of the strips of reed used for casting lots or gaming. In the present time Egyptians throw half a dozen slips of reed on the ground, and count how many fall with outside upward, to give a number as with dice. The inner side of this slip, which was probably one of a set, is carved with a bound captive. The work is excellent, as may be seen in the photographs xii. 12, 13. The plaited lock hanging down, the form of the beard, and the face, all agree to this being a western man or Libyan. But the long waist-cloth seems hardly to be expected at a time when, as the slates and ivory carvings of Hierakonpolis show,

clothing was not much developed. This is good evidence for the usual waist-cloth of the Old Kingdom being Libyan in origin.

23. THE SEALINGS, pls. xii., xviii. to xxix. The general appearance of the caps of clay which were used to fasten the jars is shown in the photographs xii. 3, 4, 5, 6; and the jars, as found intact, in photograph xxxviii. 7. The mouth of a jar was first covered with a stopper of pottery; the jar was put in a network of rope (shown in the figures of jars on seal xxi. 29); and then a dome cap (as xii. 3) or a high cone (as xii. 4, 6) of yellowish clay mixed with palm fibre was plastered over the top, and this was sealed by rolling a cylinder seal across it twice at right angles. Sometimes the two impressions are of the same seal (as seen in xii. 3), sometimes they are of different seals. There were often two sealings; at first a smaller cone sealed across, and then a coat of about ½-inch thick of more clay, and a second sealing upon that. Thus often a quite illegible cone may yet yield a good inscription by carefully knocking away an outer coat. In no case did I find a difference in the reign of the two coats; on the contrary, the second coat was put on before the first one was hard. These cones are usually marked with several rough scores on them, put on quite regardless of the impression of the seals (seen on a middle one in xxxviii. 7); and often a row of finger holes. These markings are probably a tally of quantities, and were all put on while the clay was moist.

Besides these sealings on yellow clay there were many upon ordinary black Nile mud; they are much softer, and more difficult to read; fortunately some have been baked in the burning, and are better preserved. The forms are never high cones, sometimes dome caps, but more usually almost or quite flat. Beside these are a few seals on cords which have tied up packets or the lids of jars, as seen at Medum (*Med.*, xiii.). These black clay seals are the more important historically, as they alone give

the *suten biti* names of the kings. In no case is there aught but a *ka* name on the great yellow cones; but on black mud sealings we have the joint names of Den-Setui (on a very fragmentary impression not here drawn, as I hope for others in clearing the tomb in future), of Azab-Merpaba, xxvi. 57, and of Mersekha-Semempses, xxviii. 72.

The copies here were generally compiled from several examples, sometimes ten or twelve would assist in giving the complete impression. Nothing is here inserted except from actual impressions, but a few dotted lines. A blank or imperfect sign means that so far I have not seen that identical part, however certain its reading may be by repetition. The number of repetitions around the seal were carefully sought by observing minute differences; and where the extent of repetition was uncertain the drawing is left without end lines, as in No. 37.

The material of the original cylinder seals was probably wood. On some impressions is a raised line running from top to bottom across the signs, and therefore accidental. This could only be produced by a split in the seal, and such is very likely to occur in wood. The cylinders were from 1·6 to 3·3 inches long, and up to as much as 2½ inches diameter.

I do not attempt to enter on details of the readings, as Mr. Griffith will deal with them in his account, but only make a few notes on archaeological points. The sealings are numbered continuously, so that the plate numbers need not be noted.

24. THE SEAL INSCRIPTIONS, pls. xviii. to xxix. 2, 3. The placing of *ath* ⟨⟩ with the name of Zet may be connected with the name presumably equivalent with Zet, ⟨⟩, in the Table of Abydos.

4. The doors here show the pivot and top pin, as on the piece of pottery, vii. 9. The fortress is the same as in the following No. 5.

6. The figure of the swimmer here in the canal is the first and most natural of a series.

In 18 it is clumsy, and the figure also appears out of the water (see also 20, 21). In 46 the figure is without the canal. In 67, 69 it is more conventional; and lastly, in 81, the swimmer is quite apart from the water, without even the drops of spray.

8, 9, 10. These seals are very different in character from the others, far coarser and more irregular. They are probably survivals of an older style.

11. This piece of accounts, written on the base of a brown pottery dish, is the oldest that is known. It seems to refer to quantities of things rather than to individuals; as the numbers, though mostly 20, are sometimes 100 and 220.

12, 13, 14, 15, 18. In all these occurs the *ka* arms holding a throw-stick or wand, a sign which comes from earlier times (see No. 10), but which disappeared afterwards.

21—27. A difficulty occurs in the sealings from the tomb of Merneit, that not one bears the name of Merneit, and many have the name of Den. Yet it will be seen that the seals are quite different from those of the tomb of Den. Not one is in common. Moreover, there are many peculiarities of Merneit's seals, such as the *ad mer* Seta, Nos. 24, 25; the vineyard, No. 31; the place of the boar, No. 33; the ram, No. 34; the corn measures (?), 37, 38, 39; the nomes of the east and the west, 37, 38; and the *sezet hotep* fortress, 40, 41; and not one of these occurs on any seal belonging to the tomb of Den. On the other hand, the peculiarities of Den, as the *sekhent du Hor* building, and the frequent name of *Hemaka*, bearer of the seal, never occur on the sealings from Merneit.

We cannot therefore look on these sealings as having been all made by officials of King Den. Rather must we suppose that Merneit had the name Den, and that it was adopted by his successor, the well-known king Den-Setui. It is possible that in No. 26 we might read Merneit,

as the second sign might be another form of the distaff without the arrows.

33. The "place of the boar" occurs again under Azab, better engraved in No. 60. The object over the boar, or over the jars in No. 60, looks like a brick-mould with its handle, but might be the sign *sekher*.

34. The ram following *mer-se-khnum* appears to be on a different stand in each repetition; though not in clear condition, the four forms cannot be the same.

37, 38, 39. A cylindrical vessel with two handles in these seals seems to be a measure for corn or dry goods. The two seals 37, 38 are a pair, one for the produce of the east, the other of the west. On 39 the sign of Neit appears, but no *mer*.

43. The large object shown on this seems, from the more detailed seal 86, to represent a shrine of a sacred bird.

45—50 show the name of the fortress or tomb of Den, *Hor-se-khent-du*: this was not intelligible in the drawing by De Morgan, 784.

47, 54. The two forms of jars, wide and narrow, shown here with their sealings upon them, are the two types of early jars, the pointed, as in xxxix. 5, and the full, as in xl. 11.

53—56. Hemaka was the royal seal-bearer, apparently vizier of that time (see xv. 16, 17). Some small sealings from Den and from W 33 are drawn enlarged on pl. xxxii., Nos. 38-41 (see pl. xii. 7).

57—60. The seals of Azab show a distinct advance in detail and arrangement. The palace of the *Hor-pa-ua* is named, confirming the conclusion from the stone vase inscriptions, that this name referred to the royal living palace. All these with *suten biti* are on black mud.

71. This piece of ivory carving might have appeared better on pl. xv. It seems to have been part of the inlaying of a casket or of furniture. The two Hathor heads recall those on the great slate of Narmer (see photograph, xi. 13).

72. This important seal, which fixes the identity of Mersekha, occurs on two small lumps of clay, each bearing a few very partial prints of it. They were used to fasten the knot of two cords; and the inscription seems to belong to some material for cleansing the mouth.

73, 74 are difficult to read, owing to their very imperfect state; these, as well as 72, bearing the *suten biti* title are on black mud. The buildings named on them begin with *suten biti*, but there is nothing following that can be made any equivalent of "Semempses" or of the figure on 72. They must probably be all titles of the king, the "golden bull."

77. This seal is interesting, as we have precisely the same seal in the tomb of Qa, excepting that the name of the king has been cut out, and there is therefore a mere lump in place of it on the impression. This shows that after a king's death his official seals could not be used, or at least must have his name erased if no other seal was provided.

86. This delicately cut seal has the same shrine on it, with a couchant jackal and feather over it, as we see on the stele of Sabef, pl. xxx.

87, 88. These two sealings of Perabsen were found by accident in clearing the grave W 30, at the end of the cemetery close to the tomb of Perabsen. This group of graves is not of his date, as in W 33 was the bowl of Azab, vi. 8. Doubtless more seals of Perabsen and of other kings will be found in exploring their tombs next year.

25.—THE STELES, Frontispiece, pls. xxx. to xxxvi. The principal stele found was the great one of Merneit, a king hitherto unknown (see frontispiece). His place in the Dynasty seems to have been immediately after Zet, and before Den; and the style of this stele, its size, and material, all agree well to this date. The emblem of Neit here is apparently the distaff, with two arrows across it; and this explains such a sign which occurs on a seal, 39, and on

some of the black steatite cylinders of very early age. The hoe, *mer*, and the mouth, *r*, complete the inscription. The block is about five feet high; the lower part left in the rough hammer-dressing, the upper part scraped smooth. Just above the ground level, below the inscription, the surface is scaled, owing to soaking up damp from the ground; higher up it is sand-polished. This grand stele is now, of course, kept at Cairo. In the tomb were parts of a fellow stele; the rough back (lxiv. 6), the lower part of the face up to the bottom of the *neit* sign, and the top showing just the rounding of the top of the *neit* sign: all the rest had perished.

There was also found a stele of Qa, in black quartzose rock, like that figured by De Morgan, fig. 779. In this second example the edges had been broken all around, so that the panelling of the false door is lost, but the whole hawk and name is perfect. Being difficult to move, it was not photographed at first, and later on we ran short of plates, so it will be published next year.

The best private stele found is that of Sabef, pl. xxx. and xxxvi. 48. This lay in a chamber on the west of Qa, here marked with the name on the plan, pl. lx. The block has been ground all over, with rounded edges, and not square in angles. The inscription was then sketched on it with red ink, finally drawn in black ink (represented by a full tint on pl. xxx.), and then the ground was roughly hammered out. There the work stopped, and the final scraping and dressing was never done. Hence it is difficult—if not impossible—to settle what the forms of some signs were intended to be; and the red and black ink traces are valuable for showing some details. We see that Sabef was the keeper of the tomb, *Ha Sa-ha-neb*; of the palace, *Ha Hor-pa-va*; companion in the royal palace; had two other titles that are not clear; and lastly was overseer of the Sed festival. All this shows how little the official titles moved between the Ist Dynasty and the pyramid times. This stele remains at the Cairo Museum. On pl. xxxi. I have transcribed all the steles that I found, as often the details cannot be all seen in one lighting in a photograph. The photographs of all these are given in pls. xxxiii,—xxxvi., with the same numbers, and the transcripts are arranged as on those four plates, for convenience of reference.

As it is important to be able to compare all of such material together, I have further sketched on pl. xxxii. all the steles found in this cemetery by the Mission Amelineau, so far as anything can be discerned in the photographs published; for some I have had the help of M. De Morgan's drawings, and notes of my own. But I disclaim any profession of certainty about these copies; they are merely for convenience of reference, and the only authority is in the published photographs.

The small steles can be best appreciated from the photographs, pls. xxxiii.—xxxvi. They are in all conditions from a perfectly fresh state, as No. 3, down to a trace scarcely legible even in the best light, as No. 31. But those which seem to have kept their original position longest, and neither to have buried the face, or left it upturned to the weather, show the proofs that these stones were set upright, like the great royal steles, with about a quarter of the length in the ground. No. 17 shows a great amount of sand wear on both sides of the upper part, and then within $\frac{1}{4}$ of an inch it changes to a perfect fresh unaltered surface, slightly stained by burial.

The earlier steles of the reign of Zet are much simpler, usually only one or two signs, as Nos. 1-5. There we see Neit on three steles from Z and W, 9, 10, 11, probably of the age of king Merneit: also on one stele, 20, from Den. The name Setui appears on No. 21 from the tomb of Den. The mere outlining style 23, 24, first appears under the reign of Den. The flint knife on No. 24 is excellently done, with

exactly the curve and handle of the knives of the beginning of this Dynasty. The two steles of dwarfs, 36, 37, should be noted; the name *nefert* seems to have been thought fitting, showing that in early use the word had rather a sense of mere pleasing or amusement than any aesthetic idea of beauty. The title on 40 seems to be the same as in the second line of the stele of Sabef. I do not enter on any details of the signs, as I have already shown how I should read them in the transcriptions pl. xxxi.

26. THE SMALL OBJECTS. It is not possible to make any description in detail of the innumerable fragments of wood, ivory, stone, gold and copper found in the graves, until the collection can be deliberately worked over in England. Selections of the more intelligible pieces from each tomb were photographed, and are reproduced on pl. xxxvii.

Many pieces of ivory legs of caskets were found, mostly so decomposed that they fell into flakes; but two were in sound state, and are given on pl. xii. 8, 9. They show a sense of the use of conventional art in the veining which is very advanced, and looks more like cinquecento Italian work than like anything archaic.

The strange fragment, xii. 10, is quite inexplicable; the relief marks are delicately and clearly cut, and along the lower edge is a finished notching.

The copper bowl, xii. 11, is roughly hammered, and with the edge turned over to finish it. It shows that some still rougher copper vessels which come from Abydos probably belong to the opening of the Ist Dynasty or earlier.

Pl. xxxvii. 1 is a toilet dish, carved in two halves out of a single block of ivory, each in form of half a duck with the tails interlocked. It was found in a tomb with over a dozen stone vases (yet to be published) and large pottery jars (xxxix. 1, 3, 4, 9, 10, 16-19, 50, 51, and 78). From the forms of the pottery this appears to belong to the beginning of the Ist Dynasty.

The tomb was in the temenos of Osiris, close to our house, and was found by accident.

2—14 are from cemetery W. 2. A hair-pin with degraded bird type. 3. Edge of a dish with rope border. 4. Carving of a reed with knots. 5. The hand of a small ivory statuette. 6. Part of an ivory dish with rope border. 7, 9. Parts of ivory cylinder jars, with wavy line. 8, 11, 12. Pieces of ivory inlaying. 10. Copper wire. 13, 14. Ivory points of arrows; the same form in hard wood is actually found on prehistoric arrows.

15—28 are from the cemetery of Merneit. 15, 16 are pieces of carved ivory furniture. 17. The leg of a casket in hard wood. 18—25. Pieces of carved ivory from boxes and furniture. 26 is a piece of carved slate; the great variety of carved slate is left to be worked up in future. 27, 27A. A piece of a dish in form of a hand, in alabaster. 28. One of several pieces of serpentine vases, with rope network patterns.

29—36 are from the tomb of Den-Setui. 29, 30, 32. Pieces of ivory inlay. 31. Piece of thick ivory carved as a bundle of reeds. 33. Wood carving of a reed with joints. 34. Ivory. 35. A copper harpoon. 36. Piece of an ivory cylinder jar with wavy band.

37—46 are from the tomb of Mersekha. 37. A copper borer, quadrangular, with a tang turned over. 38. Copper tweezers, of excellent pattern, with stiff ends, still in perfect order. 39, 42 and 43. Pieces of blue glazed pottery. 40, 41. Copper foil, from bindings. 44. Wood with raised pattern filled with inlay. 45. Wood carved with network pattern. 46. Wood carved with feather pattern.

47—60 are from around the tomb of Azab. 47—54. Pieces of ivory inlay from boxes. 55. A strip of ivory with the pattern so well known on early false doors of the Old Kingdom, its source yet unexplained. 56, 57. Ivory. 58-60. Violet-blue glazed pottery.

61—78 from tomb of Mersekha. 61. Ivory inlay. 62. Beetle-like object in ivory. 63. Legs in ivory. 64-5. Ribbed ivory. 66-7. Ivory carvings of bundles of reeds. 68-74. Ivory inlaying. 75. Wood with signs, three fingers (see Ivory, xvi. 21). 76. Wood carving of a mat of papyrus bound with string. 77, 78. Pieces of a wooden funeral bier (?) carved with pattern of matting; on these are cloth attached, and traces of silver objects. 79. A piece of ivory from the tomb of Qa; much more of this pattern was found partly decayed; the pieces have tenons on the back to fit into a base, and probably it was part of a bier of wood, encrusted with ivory, carved to represent a reed mat.

Pl. xxxviii. 1 is a fragment of a vase in very hard grey marble, carved as the calyx of a flower. 2 is part of another calyx vase, carved in crystal. 3 is a model of a water-skin, found in many pieces about the tomb of Mersekha. 4 is the lower part of an alabaster cylinder jar, with *uas* signs around it. 5, 6 are some of the rough limestone models of vases, painted in imitation of marble, found in a box in the grave Q 20, by the tomb of Qa. In 8 are an alabaster cylinder jar and bowl and a slate bowl, from the grave Q 21; the only perfect stone vases that we found. 9 is a piece of pottery with the peculiar dressing characteristic of the earliest pottery at Lachish; it is important, as the form of the wavy handles of prehistoric vases is also very characteristic of this earliest Palestine pottery, and therefore some connection is probable.

27. THE POTTERY, pls. xxxix. to xliii. The great quantity of drawing requisite for the sealings and ivories left me but little time for the pottery; so that only a part of it is here figured, and more will be published next year.

Of the large jars the type 2 is perhaps the earliest; the three rings on it retain a rope pattern, and from the position of its grave B 1 to the east of Zer, it is likely that the hawk on it is a corrupted form of the hawk with shield and club of king Aha. Of about the same time are

Nos. 2 and 3 from the grave M 1. The degradation of form down to the type 7 found in the tomb of Q is quite distinct.

Another type was the fatter jar without rings. The earliest of these from B 1 has a trace of the old wavy handle of the prehistoric on its shoulder. This form seems to have continued through the dynasty. The ring-stands 13, 14, 15, are well developed, and would lead up to the narrow waisted type at Dendereh in the IIIrd Dynasty.

The jars 16—31 are rounder than the prehistoric types from which they come (*Naqada*, xl. 36, 38); later on more neck was developed in the IVth Dynasty (*Dendereh*, xvi. 21, 26, *Medum*, xxx. 11).

The jars to stand without a ring, 53—55, agree with the Medum type (xxxi. 20), and apparently come from the prehistoric (*Naqada*, xli. 94).

The small jars 56—64 are usually red faced and burnished, and often have inscriptions. They come from the prehistoric type (*Naqada*, xli. 53); and with narrower necks, but yet with burnished red face, they last to the VIth Dynasty, as in *Dendereh*, xvi. 11, 12, 13, also having inscriptions.

The awkward forms, 65, 66, come from the prehistoric (*Naq.*, xli. 53), but after the wheel was introduced the shoulder and neck were made separate from the body and pieced on.

The upright libation vase 110 seems entirely dynastic. The neck rapidly disappeared, and the body lengthened, until in the tomb of Qa are innumerable cylinders of red pottery, which are the stems of such jars.

The old type of the cylinder jar, descended from prehistoric times, can be seen steadily degrading further in the series, 119—129, until it passed into quite a different form by the end of the dynasty.

The very thick bowls with rough bottom, 145—151, are well known in the IVth Dynasty, of the type 151: see *Medum*, xxxi. 17; *Den-*

dereh, xvi. 14, 15. The meaning of this form is that a hole was scooped in the ground or dust, a lump of mud was laid in it, and then trimmed and wiped round by hand until it formed a thick clumsy bowl. This was left to dry in the sun, and then picked up and baked. Thus the outside is always quite rough below, and the thickness is disproportionate.

28. THE MARKS ON POTTERY, pls. xliv. to lviii. Most of the large jars bear marks, which were scratched in the moist clay before being baked; some few were marked after the baking. These are not always the same way upward, some having been marked with the hand below the mark, others from above. The classification of these marks is needful, and the publication of the whole of them, in order to judge of their sources. Some are unquestionably hieroglyphs; others are probably connected with the signs used by the earlier prehistoric people; and many can scarcely be determined.

The copies here published are all reduced to one-third from drawings made in Egypt by my wife, who has arranged them here, and studied the interpretation of several as described here. An impression of the incised mark was taken on paper, and the drawing made over it, so as to ensure its exactness. The order here is according to the nature of the marks, the examples of each mark being classed chronologically. The reference letters are those used for denoting the tombs throughout the work; their meaning can be seen on the plan, pl. lix. Where the source of a jar was uncertain both letters are given; thus many were of either U or Q, and these are marked UQ. The groups 1 to 9, marked B, come from a private tomb to the east of that of Zer, near where a jar sealing and a bracelet of Aha-Mena were found; they are, therefore, probably the oldest here.

Pl. xliv. 1. This tail of a fish seems to be part of a *ka* name; if so, it belongs to some yet unknown king, probably before Mena.

2—9. These large figures of hawks are of

the earliest type, like those of Narmer and Aha. No. 731 is probably the same. As the locality points to these being of the age of Aha it seems not unlikely that these are corruptions of the Aha hawk holding the shield and club. The jars are shown in xxxix. 2 ; xl. 8.

10—110. The whole of these must be considered together, as they may be entirely copies of one inscription more or less degraded. The best examples, such as 11, 12, 16, 20, 21 seem to be distinctly of Mersekha. The fortified enclosure around the name may refer to the tomb, as the eternal fortress of the king. An imperceptible gradation of corruption leads through the forms 13, 14, where the *kha* is drawn as an oval with spots ; through 25, 26, where the panelling below the inscription is made into a square and the *kha* into a *neb;* through 44, where the *mer* and *se* are made alike ; and so to the rough scrawl of oval signs as 75, and even these signs alike as in 72. Looking at the extreme ignorance and carelessness of the marking it seems unlikely that we should give any importance to such variations as in 71, 77—80, which might be supposed to show some other name. The source of these jars agrees well to their being of Mersekha-Semempses ; 100 of them are found in his tomb, or between that and the tomb of Qa, 3 are found in Z, 1 in T, 1 in X, and 5 in Q : all these latter seem to have merely been scattered by accident, as none were discovered undisturbed.

111—156. All of these seem to be intended for the same inscription, which is given on the stone vases, viii. 11, 12 ; ix. 1 to 4 ; and also on the stele, xxx. The place *Sa ha neb* we have already noted (p. 21) is probably the name of the tomb of king Qa. The various forms on the stones are 1 of *Hor·ha·sa,* 3 of *Sa ha·neb,* 1 of *Sa·neb·ha.* On the pottery it is, however, in every case *Ha·sa* only, agreeing with the *Hor·ha·sa* of viii. 11. The form also of a tablet on steps is like that on the stone. But these names on pottery are scattered over nearly all

the cemetery : taking only those which clearly show the order of signs there are 2 from W (age of Zet ?), 2 from Merneit, 4 from Den, 14 from Azab, 3 from Mersekha, 5 of him or Qa, and 3 from Qa. No doubt some may be merely scattered, but as most of them are found far from Qa they cannot all be attributed to the tomb of Qa, to which the *Sa·ha·neb* stone bowls belong. Hence we must rather regard the *Sa·ha* as being the generic name of the tomb in the Ist Dynasty, which was used by Qa specifically, with *neb* added to it.

Pl. xlvii. begins the known hieroglyphs of human form. 159 is a man standing, possibly a variant of Mersekha, as it comes from the next tomb to his. 160—162 and 838 (?) seem possibly intended for the sacred emblem of Osiris at Abydos ; the head, or rather wig, which is shown so often in the temple, as the object of adoration in the sacred bark, and also as the *ab* hieroglyph in the name Abdu=Abydos. The usual printed forms of that sign *ab* are absurd ; the best examples in the great temple show a wig on a stand, sometimes with a head fillet around it, and the uraeus rising from that, surmounted by the double feather.

163—168 show the *ka* arms on legs. 169 the disc and wings and *ka* arms, carrying back this emblem from the IVth Dynasty (Khufu, *Hist.,* i. 38) to the Ist. Possibly Nos. 253, 483—485 are the same.

170, 171 is perhaps the *her* head, as it is drawn with a very short neck on the stele, xxxii. 13.

172—187, *neter ka,* the divine ka ; none later than Azab. The sign *neter* is always drawn with a double top in this original form, as on the ivories xiii. 2, xiv. 12A, and the stele xxxii. 8, and cannot therefore be an axe.

188—207, *ka* with a disc, sometimes with strokes across it, as in 190, 192, 193 ; probably all of Mersekha, a few having strayed to Den, Merneit, and Qa. 208, *ka* and *du,* double hill sign. 209—236, *ka* with a forked sign ; 237 —249, *ka* with a square. These second signs may not be hieroglyphs. 250—280, various signs with *ka*, of which only 260, 264, 265, 270 seem to have a hieroglyph, the hoe. 281—339, *ka* arms, with and without a stroke. 340—344, seem to be the *ka* arms and stroke combined.

345—376, the wavy lines with the *ka* appear in the best examples to be intended for serpents (see Nos. 423—427). With these we may compare the two serpents in shrines figured in the XIIth Dynasty (see *Koptos*, ix. 2, before head of Min).

Pl. xlix. contains the animal figures. 377—386 are various quadrupeds. 387—395 are perhaps intended for a jerboa or lizard. The birds 396—410 cannot be safely discriminated, as the early forms are uncertain even in good work.

411—413 are of the *zet* serpent. Next are the double serpents 414—421, and then single serpents 422—433. As so often two or more signs are found placed together, it is impossible to group every example of a sign in one place ; hence, classing by the most important or distinctive sign, some—such as the double serpent—appear in several plates.

435—482 are fish with two serpents and squares. Those with serpents are all of Zet and Merneit ; the ordinary type of fish are never found in the tomb of Merneit.

Pl. L. contains hieroglyph marks. 483-4 are the sun and wings with *neb*. 485 the same with *mer neter*. 486—505 *neter*, with various other signs. 506—510 the three-hill sign *set* ; this and other signs appear inverted because such were drawn with the hand next to the mouth of the jar, probably by a man leaning over the jar as it rested against his knees. None of the marks are here turned round, as it is right to show strictly what way they stand when the jar is mouth upwards. 511—533 are two-hill signs, *du* ; the general sign occurring with them being a circle.

534 is the sickle, *ma*.

535—567 the hoe *mer*, the general sign occurring with it being the fork, in Nos. 540 to 546.

568—574, apparently the *hotep*, mat and offering. 575-7 the *sa* cord. 578 marked on a clay jar cap ; the forepart of a lion, *hat*, or the forepart of an ibis, with probably *ha* or perhaps *sha* plants.

579—584, a curious group which can hardly be explained as hieroglyphs. The narrow signs might be *mer's* ; the other object is seen in Nos. 585—589, and perhaps 593.

594—604, various forms of the *qema* or *resi* plant sign ; always drawn with the finger before baking ; perhaps to denote southern wine.

605—668, crescent and star accompanied by *neter*, *mer*, T, divided disc, and square.

29. THE SIGNARY, pl. lii. Here we reach signs which seem to be disconnected from the known hieroglyphs, and in the following plates we are probably touching on the system of geometrical signs used from prehistoric to Roman times in Egypt, and also in other countries around the Mediterranean. How far these signs are originally due to geometrical invention, or how far due to corruption of some picture, we cannot say. But in any case they stood so detached from the hieroglyphic writing and its hieratic and demotic derivations, that they must be treated as a separate system. For the present the best course is to show here the similarity of forms between these marks and those known in Egypt in earlier and later times ; adding the similar forms in the Karian and Spanish alphabets. The usage of such forms in the same country from about 6000 B.C. down to 1200 B.C. or later, shows that we have to deal with a definite system. And it seems impossible to separate that in 1200 B.C. in Egypt from the similar forms found in other lands connected with Egypt from 800 B.C. down to later times ; we may find many of these also in the Kretan inscriptions long before 800 B.C.

The only conclusion then seems to be that a great body of signs—or a *signary*—was in use around the Mediterranean for several thousand years. Whether these signs were ideographic or syllabic or alphabetic in the early stages we do not know; certainly they were alphabetic in the later stage. And the identity of most of the signs in Asia Minor and Spain shows them to belong to a system with commonly received values in the later times.

What then becomes of the Phoenician legend of the alphabet? Certainly the so-called Phoenician letters were familiar long before the rise of Phoenician influence. What is really due to the Phoenicians seems to have been the selection of a short series (only half the amount of the surviving alphabets) for numerical purposes, as $A = 1$, $E = 5$, $I = 10$, $N = 50$, $P = 100$, $\Phi = 500$, &c. This usage would soon render these signs as invariable in order as our own numbers, and force the use of them on all countries with which the Phoenicians traded. Hence, before long these signs drove out of use all others, except in the less changed civilizations of Asia Minor and Spain. This exactly explains the phenomena of the early Greek alphabets; many in variety, and so diverse that each has to be learned separately, and yet entirely uniform in order. Each tribe had its own signs for certain sounds, varying a good deal; yet all had to follow a fixed numerical system. Certainly all did not learn their forms from an independent Phoenician alphabet, unknown to them before it appeared as a whole. The history of the alphabet is as old as civilization.

30. A few words of explanation of Heqreshu hill are needed. It is called the first butte by M. Amélineau, but it has no connection with the royal tombs. The oldest remains found there are pieces of a sculptured tomb of the Vth Dynasty, of a man named Emzaza. Nothing can be dated there after that until the XVIIIth Dynasty. At that time, with the revived interest in the kings' tombs, this rise became venerated: very possibly the ruins of the mastaba of Emzaza were mistaken for a royal tomb. It was the custom for persons buried elsewhere—probably at Thebes—to send down a very fine

Comparative table of signs (glyphs) with the column headings:

EGYPT Prehis.	EGYPT Ist Dyn.	EGYPT XIIth Dyn.	EGYPT XVIII D.	KARIA	(value)	SPAIN
					a	
					ä	
					e	
					e	
					e	
					ê	
					â	
					ai	
					i	
					i	
					i	
					o	
					u	
					w	
					bh	
					b	
					g	
					d	
					v	
					z	
					kh	
					th	
					dh	
					k	
					l	
					m	
					m	
					n	
					p	
					r	
					s	
					s	
					sh	
					t	
					h	
					vu	
					re	
					rd	
					kh	
					kh	
					ki	

ushabti to be buried here, often accompanied by bronze models of yokes and baskets and hoes, for the ushabti to work with in the kingdom of Osiris. The finest of these ushabtis were three of Heqreshu, from whom we named the hill; one is of white marble, exquisitely wrought, another of solid blue glass, both banded with gold foil, a third of ebony; the bronze baskets with these were incised with the name. All these are now in Cairo. The most important after these was one in solid bronze, of a royal scribe Any, probably the person whose great papyrus is in the British Museum. All of these ushabtis will be published with the later historical things next year. A limestone base of a figure covered with adorations roughly incised was also found here. The whole hillock is strewn with pieces of broken offering jars.

CHAPTER IV.

THE INSCRIPTIONS.

By F. Ll. Griffith, M.A., F.S.A.

31. In the plates to this volume Professor Petrie has far more than doubled the materials available for studying the earliest known period of writing in Egypt; they now afford us a considerable insight into the condition of that art at and about the time of the Ist Dynasty. Egyptian writing developed rapidly during the Old Kingdom; the beginning of the IVth Dynasty was especially a period of rapid improvement, and it has long been recognised that the graffiti of Khufu are written with considerable freedom. It is, however, somewhat startling to find cursive writing in the time of the Ist Dynasty. Some of the scratched signs on vases in these plates are very much abbreviated, but it is the ink-writing which here, as elsewhere at all periods, displays the most remarkable development. Nos. 3, 4, 5 on Pl. x. show "linear hieroglyphs" scarcely distinguishable from those of much later periods: more particularly is this the case with the in No. 5; and the form of the accounts in Pl. xix., No. 11, is not less striking.

Another fact which it is interesting to observe is that, with one exception, all the essential features of the Egyptian system of writing appear well developed at this remote period. The rapid change from the inscriptions at the end of the IIIrd Dynasty to those of the IVth Dynasty would have prepared us to find some radical difference in the writing of the Ist Dynasty. But apparently no such difference exists in fact; at present, indeed, we find no clear evidence of the employment of determinative signs in these primitive writings, but even as late as the Vth Dynasty their use was very restricted in the monumental writing, though it was common in the cursive, and in the freely written texts of the Pyramids. As more specimens of cursive writing come to light of this very early period, we may expect to ascertain with certainty that the use of determinatives had already begun. Though and and are probably to be read in most cases as word-signs for z·t, ḥ·t, most of the alphabetic signs are already in full use as simple phonograms, and their employment as "phonetic complements" is likewise well established. Thus ⌒ t constantly accompanies ⌡, e.g in ⌐⌐ ⌡, ix. 2, to distinguish its value as stn from its other value, sw; and the same sign stands separately for the feminine ending of by·t, "bee," in by·ty, "King of Lower Egypt," lit. "He that belongs to the Bee," or perhaps "the Bee-keeper." But though the system was developed, it must not be supposed that writing was as easy then as it was in the time of the XIIth Dynasty and later. The full and more or less fixed spelling of later writing provided so many checks to the reading that a practised scribe need seldom mistake the meaning of a passage, even when taken at random. In the early part of the Old Kingdom this was not so, and under the Ist Dynasty it would seem that one sign to a word was the usual allowance. The reading, therefore, depended on the exact recognition of each individual sign. When the characters were carefully made the scribe would generally recognise the meaning from them alone; but if they were at all cursive the writing would rather seem to help the memory or perception of something very simple, or already half known, than to record the unexpected with exactness and fidelity. Nearly all the early texts as yet discovered consist of mere names and titles. Few have been found that might display syntactical construction. An example on pl. x. (xvi. 20) suggests that the less important words in a sentence might be dropped out, at least in "pictorial" hieroglyphic—the term by which most Egyptian inscriptions may be designated—of that period. Written in this way a long text would only be intelligible with the help of traditional interpreters. The variant texts of religious works in later times are probably often due to the obscurities and ambiguities of very early originals.

Professor Petrie has already drawn from these inscriptions the interesting historical names which they contain, and other details. There can no longer be a shadow of doubt that the bulk of them belong to the earliest kings in the Abydos list of Sety I., corresponding to the Ist Dynasty of Manetho.

32. Since the inscriptions consist so largely of royal names, it is worth while to consider the significance of the different titles which accompany the names of kings. From the Vth Dynasty onwards the full royal protocol shows five distinct titles, each followed by a name, as follows:—

1. The title "Horus" 𓅃. Usually the hawk is perched on a building, above the façade of which the special name of the king is engraved. This title is probably to be connected with Osiris worship, and indicates that the king was the living successor and son of Osiris on earth, his father being in the Underworld.

2. The title 𓎢 *Nb·ty*, "the Two Mistresses," i.e., first, the Mistress of Upper Egypt and the South generally, the vulture goddess Nekhebt of El Kab; secondly, the Mistress of Lower Egypt and the North, the uraeus goddess Uazyt of Buto. This title no doubt means that the king represents the two goddesses and is invested with their authority.

3. The title 𓅉 *Ḥrw nb*, "Golden Horus"; of obscure significance, but rendered in the Greek text of the Rosetta Stone by ἀντιπάλων ὑπέρτερος, "victorious (?) over his enemies." "Golden" may thus here indicate superiority over other hawks. It is worth noting that Ch. lxxvii. of the Book of the Dead prescribes how to "assume the form of a great Hawk of Gold."

4. The title 𓇓𓆤 *stn·y by·ty*, "King of the South and North," or "of Upper and Lower Egypt"; probably a compound of two ancient titles once held separately (*Hieroglyphs*, p. 29; *Ptahhetep* I., p. 23), but in mythological texts especially held by the Sun-god as being in heaven and over the whole universe. The name following it (in and after the Vth Dynasty) always connects the king with the Sun-god Ra. It may be called the dual-kingdom title.

5. The title 𓅭𓇳 *s' R'*, "son of the Sun," i.e., legitimate successor of Ra, preceding the personal name of the king.

The last two titles, essentially solar after the Vth Dynasty, are enclosed in "cartouches" 𓍷. This figure, named *šnnw* in Egyptian (*Hieroglyphs*, p. 47), probably signifies the orbit of the sun as the theoretical boundary to the realm of the king whose name was inscribed within it; just as the Horus-name was inscribed within or on the representation of the palace to show who was its possessor.

The title 𓅭𓇳 (5) was probably not introduced before the Vth Dynasty, but all the other titles are found in the IVth Dynasty, at which time 𓇓𓆤 was followed by the personal name in a cartouche. In the Ist Dynasty apparently there is no "cartouche," nor does the Golden Horus title (3) occur. The employment of the titles also is variable. It can hardly be doubted that Mer-Neit (pl. i.) was a king, yet no title nor any other name for him has yet been discovered. Usually, however, the Horus (1) and Ra (4) titles are found, and in most cases the Nebty title (2) as well in some form. Of these (4) and (2) are commonly associated and precede a single name, and (1) is separate. For 𓈖𓃥 some earlier (?) kings have ▽ ▽ alone, which would read *Nb·ty* as before, unless it be *Nb·wy*, "the two masters," meaning Horus and Set, the gods of Lower and Upper Egypt. The latter is certainly the meaning of 𓃝 𓃝 *Ntr·wy*, "the two gods," in the inscriptions of Merpaba.

Note by Professor Petrie.

As the subject of the royal titles is mentioned it may be as well to state some of the views which I have reached in recent years; such observations are generally too piece-meal to be worth stating immediately. The five titles detailed by Mr. Griffith seem to me to belong to the lordship of different tribes or stages of the kingdom, like the long compound territorial titles of the Prince of Wales—Duke of Cornwall, Duke of Rothesay, &c., &c.; or the King of Sweden, Norway, the Goths and Vandals; or the Emperor of all the various Russias and Grand Duke of Finland.

1. The *ka* name appears to belong to the dynastic race; it is by far the most usual title in the Ist Dynasty, and it always took precedence of the others. The addition of the hawk—the king's soul—on the top is later, as it is generally absent in Narmer (before Mena); it seems to have been added to convey the idea that this was the name of the king to eternity, and not adopted as a territorial name. As Osiris is a Libyan god, and belongs to an older stratum of population, any connection with Osiris is due to this being the eternal name, and Osiris being lord of eternity.

The frame in which this name is placed is often certainly over a doorway, as it is shown with all details of a door in various ages (*Season in Egypt*, xx.), or if not figured as the door of the tomb it is the panelled brick wall of the tomb (as here, v. 4, vi. 1, 2, 11); and the recesses and projections (scarcely to be called "towers") are like those of the tomb of Mena and Babylonian brickwork. Being the *ka* name it belongs rather to a tomb than a palace.

2. The double *neb* title is first found without any symbols over it, as in the names of kings D and Zeser (xxxii. 32, and iv. 3), which are about the age of Mena, and probably earlier rather than later. As this title belongs to the extension of the power of Upper Egypt over the Lower, it must have been formed at the time of the conquest of Lower Egypt by the dynastics.

3. The *Hor-nub* title does not occur in the Ist or IInd Dynasty, nor until the time of Shaaru and Khufu, under whom it appears as two hawks on the *nub*. It belongs, therefore to a time after the completion of the kingdom; it might refer to the conquest of the Sinai mines ("god of metal"), and the sense of "victorious over enemies" would be the secondary expression of such victories.

4. The *suten biti* is a double title, as either half occurs alone and complete. *Biti* or *bat* is undoubtedly the Libyan royal title; it interchanges with the Lower crown, which is the crown of Neit the Libyan goddess, and is found on prehistoric pottery of Libyan connection; moreover, the Libyans called a king *Battos*, as Herodotus says. As this is the Libyan or Lower Egyptian title, *suten* naturally refers to Upper Egypt; and it is probably the same plant 𓇓 as that of the sign for the South country 𓋴 (as Mr. Griffith has suggested), with a small difference to distinguish the meanings. The *suten* title is first found under Zet (xiii. 3a). It seems probable that on the absorption of the Libyan rule by the complete conquest of the Delta, the kings took over the Libyan

royal title *biti*, and then added as a correlative the name *suten*, the source of which word would indicate to which people of the south it had belonged.

5. The *si ra* title is not found until the time of the legend of the intermarriage of the royal family with the priests of Ra; it was taken over on the acquisition of the high priesthood. And thus the cartouche came to be introduced. On all the earliest and best examples the cartouche is a double cord; and it is actually seen worn as the sacred cord of the high priest on a very early statue of a high priest of Ra-Horus in the Louvre, *Ra-sankh*, before it was absorbed by the royal line. The intermarriage with the high priests of Heliopolis appears to have begun under Seneferu, the first king with a cartouche. His son Ra-hotep was high priest (*Medum*, xiii.), while his daughter conveyed the kingdom to Khufu. Again his son Merab was high priest (L., *D*., ii., xxii.*c*), while his daughter conveyed the kingdom to Khafra. By the end of the dynasty the kings united the priesthood to the kingship, and this led to their great works in honour of Ra, the Ra temples of Shepseskaf, Userkaf, and others.

6. The minor title *neb taui* is generally associated with *neter nefer*. That *taui* referred to the two banks of the Nile is shown by the example of a local prince who "made to live his *taui*" (*Hist*., i. 126); there is also the name *Ra·neb·taui*, i.e. the sun, lord of east and west, the two horizons. As this title is not early, perhaps not before Pepy, it is hardly territorial, but may have been acquired as belonging to Ra of the two horizons.

W. M. F. P.

---

33. It will be readily understood by the reader of the following comments that most of our readings are tentative, and, though many signs may be recognized clearly, the inscriptions of the Ist Dynasty still set at defiance anything like complete interpretation.

Pl. i. The hieroglyphs spelling the name of Mer-Neit in this careful sculpture are interesting. Note ⊂⊃ as the phonetic complement of *mr*. Neit (*Nt*) is represented unusually by the sign , as in Mar., *Mast*., p. 90. The arrows are feathered, and are remarkable for their chisel-shaped tips, perhaps of flint. The object figured with them may, on the analogy of the late form (as in the printed type), be a slender parrying shield. The same combination serves as the symbol of a nome of Lower Egypt, afterwards divided into the IVth or Prosopite and the Vth or Saite nomes, reading *Syp* (?) (L., *D*., ii. 3).

To find the name of a king of the Ist Dynasty compounded with that of Neith is interesting, and suggests that Sais may have been of great importance in very early times. We may here recall the fact that in inscriptions of the XXVIth (Saite) Dynasty there are constant references to a temple of Osiris that bore the significant name which probably means *H·t by·ty*, "The Residence of the King of Lower Egypt." This name may well preserve an important relic of ancient history.

It is remarkable that in all the inscriptions of Mer-Neit his name stands alone without any accompanying names or titles, as on this stela. The other royal stelae, namely, those of Zet, Mer-sech (?) and Qa-a (De Morgan, *Recherches*, ii., pp. 232, 238), give Horus names.

Pl. iv. 1. The Horus name of Menes, apparently representing the sign *ʿḥ'* "the Fighter," but with the implements of war placed in the talons of the hawk. The shield is nearly rectangular, but tapers a little below; cf. *Hieroglyphs*, fig. 177, *Medum*, pl. xii., &c. The weapon, according to Prof. Petrie, here and in all the earliest examples, is "a stone-headed pear-shaped mace" (cf. *Hieroglyphs*, p. 15).

2. The Horus name of another king; the upper sign represents a cat-fish named perhaps

$n^c r$, and the lower, here imperfect, is an unsymmetrical chisel 𓌪 *mr*. The name is therefore supposed to be $N^c r$-*mr*.

3. The sign ⌣ *Zśr*, doubtless a royal name, following the two baskets ⌣ ⌣ ; i.e., the title of the two Mistresses or Lords (?).

4. The Horus name of a king 𓆓, no doubt reading *Z·t*, "the Snake," not merely *Z*. This fuller value of the sign is found as late as the Pyramid texts of the VIth Dynasty. In *Hieroglyphs*, p. 24, I have suggested that the *zet* snake is the *Echis* or viper: but on the tablet of Menes 𓆓 replaces 𓆙, the cobra with distended hood. 𓆓 therefore probably represents the cobra, and this agrees with the drift of Horapollo's statement (i. 1) that the uraeus was immortal, eternity being likewise represented in hieroglyphics by the same word and sign, 𓆓 *z·t*. Cf. *Stories of the High Priests of Memphis*, p. 22.

This is a beautiful specimen of linear engraving. It shows the hawk of Horus perched upon an enclosure with towers in the façade (i.e., the palace), the hieroglyph composing the name being represented above the façade, i.e., either as actually over it, or more probably as in the interior of the enclosure. A king is sometimes described as 𓅃𓊖 "the Horus in the midst of the palace" (*Siut*, tomb i., l. 220). This hieroglyphic figure of the palace, as intended to bear or enclose the royal name, is termed in Egyptian 𓄟𓉔 *ś·rḫ*, meaning "that which proclaims, makes known"; and at the king's accession his "hawk" is said to "manifest itself upon the *ś·rḫ* for ever." We may contrast with this example the treatment of the same thing in the very old inscriptions of Nar-mer and Mena (Nos. 1, 2), where the form of the design shows it to have been still more or less elastic. The symbols of Mena's name are put in the talons of the hawk, and the second symbol of that of Nar-mer is thrust down between the towers of the façade. But soon the style became absolutely fixed; the hawk is perched on the edge,

and the signs are placed in a clear rectangle drawn above the façade.

5. Perhaps a private name 𓎛𓏭 *Wp-'ś·t*, Upast.

6. 𓊵 𓏏 *Ḥtp-ḥr*; probably a name, hardly the title 𓊵 of xxiv. 47, &c. Cf. perhaps xxxii. 13.

7. 𓉐𓏏𓏭𓈖 *Pr-yb-śn*, "House of their hearts (?)," a king's name, with royal titles (4) and (2). Cf. xxix. 87.

8. 𓊪𓅆𓏤. The arrow may here stand for the title 𓌕 *śwn*, "physician," followed by the name *Ywḫ*, Aukh. For the form of ⊕ with cross-hatching cf. xii. 2, xxxiv. 14, though the same sign would seem to stand for ⊗ in pl. xxii., &c. In pl. xxix. 87 ⊕ is normal.

9. Perhaps 𓄿 *ḥs* or 𓏏 *ḥśf*, or Neit sign.

10. Possibly a version of 𓏪, cf. v. 2, ix. 2-5; or 𓏪 *ḥsⁱt*.

Pl. v. 1. Mer-neit, written as on the stela; in 2-7 Neit is written with the crossed arrows alone (cf. xxxi. 9, 11), as often in O.K.; e.g. MAR., *Mast.*, 201.

2. The same with 𓉻 *pr-ḥz*, "treasury," and 𓉔 *ḥnt*.

5. The same with 𓎡𓎡 *ḥ^c-ḥ'*.

7. 𓄿 *ḥz* upon 𓉐 *ḥ·t*, "Residence," enclosing 𓉔 (?).

10. 𓎡 *^c-ḥ^c*, perhaps a name.

9, 11, 12 show the name 𓋴𓋴, preceded by the Ra title, of a king whose Horus name is ⌣ (see xv. 16). Along with them are the Horus title 𓄿 and 𓅆𓅆 and dual kingdom titles 𓇳 of another king (see xxvi. 57), added in a rather different style, contrasting especially in 12.

𓋴𓋴 is probably to be read *Sm·ty*, "Foreigner," or "Desert-man" or "Highlander." It is rendered by 𓋴𓈖(?) in the New Kingdom; this would naturally be read *Śp·ty*, but a form found in the XVIIIth Dynasty papyrus of Nu 𓋴𓈖𓋴𓋴, BUDGE, *Book of the Dead, Text*, 145, may show that this again was intended to represent *Sm·ty*, in spite of the form (▦) in Sety's list at Abydos. See SETHE in *A.Z.*, 1897, p. 3.

⟨sign⟩ is evidently ⟨cartouche⟩ of Sety's list (reading *Mr-bỉ'·p*(*w*)); cf. *id., ib.*, p. 2. It is difficult to decide whether the early spelling is to be read *Mr-pw-bỉ'* or *Mr-bỉ'-pw*, and for *pw* we might read *py* in either case. The precise meaning of the name is doubtful. The Horus name of this king (in 11) is ⟨sign⟩ *'z-yb*, "sound (or soundness) of heart."

Pl. vi. 8. *Ntr·wy* and dual kingdom titles of Merpaba, followed by ⟨sign⟩ (?) ⟨sign⟩ *qd*(?)-*htp* inscribed within ⟨sign⟩. The last sign is probably silent in such cases, and is to be treated as a kind of determinative sign. It signifies *h·t*, "Residence" (*Hieroglyphs*, p. 35). Qed-hetep may be the name of the king's tomb-city or of his Residence. The uncertain sign closely resembles ⟨sign⟩ with loop at side (*Hieroglyphs*, p. 48), of the narrow form usual in inscriptions of the IIIrd and IVth Dynasty.

Pl. vii. 1. Three plovers ⟨sign⟩, reading Rekhyt (*Ptahhetep* I., figs. 84, 410), perhaps a proper name.

2. ⟨sign⟩ *pr-bỉ'* (?) suggests that ⟨sign⟩ in the royal name may possibly mean "house of wonders." With it is the Horus title of king ⟨sign⟩, see xvii. 26. This title is written ⟨sign⟩. The first group is to be read *Ś-mr* rather than *Mr-ś*, as is shown by the similar writing of the title *śmr* in pl. xxx. The last sign, by comparison with other examples, is certainly the udder &c. ⟨sign⟩ (*Hieroglyphs*, p. 18), reading *h* as an alphabetic sign, and *h·t*, "belly," "bowels," as a word-sign. Since *h* is very rarely used in O. K. as an alphabetic sign, we may almost assume that it here has the word-sign value; and we may recall the Nebty name of Pepy I. ⟨sign⟩ "who is beloved by the *chet*." *Chet* must in such a case have been considered as the seat of the nobler feelings, and so have had the meaning of σπλάγχνον, "bowels," in the New Testament.

This meaning seems entirely lost at a later period. In the very early names the word *chet* is common; cf. *ntr h·t*, the Horus name of Tosorthros (?) of the Saqqareh Pyramid; *śb h·t Hr·w*(?), vii. 10, xxvi. 63, xxvii. 64; *Hr·w tp h·t* (?), xxv. 52, 55, 56; *Hr·w nb h·t*, xxix. 83. Here *Ś·mr-h·t* probably means "Close friend of the affections." Or *h·t* might mean "family," the sense being derived from its primitive meaning of "loins."

4. The animal at the top may be a dog or perhaps a lion. Probably it may be interpreted as the animal figure of some god, described by the compound group beneath as ⟨sign⟩ "Lord of the Residence of Life."

5. A representation of the canopy for the Sed-festival (*Hieroglyphs*, p. 36, NAVILLE, *Bubastis*, pp. 3 *et seqq.*) on a stepped base inscribed with three characters .. ⟨sign⟩ (?)

6. The sign ⟨sign⟩ "king" (erased), and ⟨sign⟩ *Hb-śd*, the name of the Sed-festival.

9. The characters ⟨sign⟩ (?) and ⟨sign⟩ (?); cf. xxxii. 33 for the third sign.

10. ★ ⟨sign⟩ (?), "Star of the family? of Horus," a place-name (?) recurring in xxvi. 63, xxvii. 64.

11. ⟨sign⟩ *Mr-śt*, possibly meaning "loving scent."

12. ⟨sign⟩ followed by an unknown sign. ⟨sign⟩ stands here for ⟨sign⟩, as in ix. 11 compared with ix. 3.

Pl. viii. 1. Dual kingdom and Nebty titles preceding the name ⟨sign⟩, which is probably to be read *Q'-'*, Qa-a, "High of hand." The Horus name of the king (2) is the same, but in 29 we have another Nebty name ⟨sign⟩ *sn*, which, as Prof. Petrie has pointed out, may well have led through its hieratic or linear forms to an erratic reading ⟨sign⟩ *Qbh* in the New Kingdom, since Qebh occurs in a corresponding place in the New Kingdom lists.

4. Signs suggestive of ⟨sign⟩ "Northern Residence."

5. See the complete example, ix. 9.

6. [hieroglyphs] perhaps *Ḥry pr-stn*, "overseer of the king's house."

7. Horus title Qa-a, accompanied by *ḥb-śd*, the latter word completed by 7*a*. See vii. 6.

8. [hieroglyphs].

9. Titles of Qa-a, and [hieroglyphs] with barge carrying stone, or boat with cabins; cf. ix. 8.

10. Tablet on stepped base, inscribed [hieroglyphs] (?), "Horus behind ... (?)," the last sign very doubtful (cf. xlvi. 121 with [hieroglyphs]); below it [hieroglyphs], evidently the word *ś‘*, "cut."

Better examples of the other inscriptions are in the following plates:—

Pl. ix. 1. Several groups, viz., *a*. [hieroglyph] containing [hieroglyphs], recurring with the signs more or less abbreviated in 2, 4, and viii. 12, "Residence of all Protection behind."

b. [hieroglyphs] "chief (?) in the king's house," or "garden-keeper of the king's house."

c. [hieroglyph] *wr*, "great," possibly belonging to the last title.

d. [hieroglyphs] *rnp·t ḥtp*, "year of peace," or perhaps "vegetables and offerings."

In 2 these titles are associated with the Horus title Qa-a.

On another part of the same vessel is a further inscription, which evidently was identical with 3, showing dual-kingdom and Nebty titles of Qa-a, and [hieroglyph] containing [hieroglyphs], perhaps meaning "The Residence of him who alone is Horus (*Ḥrw pw w‘*)," followed by the title *b*. as above, cf. xxvi. 58.

In 2 [hieroglyph] is followed by [hieroglyph], making "great one of the priestly orders (?)," and in 4 and 5 there is [hieroglyphs], "great one of the four priestly orders," preceded by [hieroglyph] Neith (?).

8. Cf. viii. 9.

12. "The sem-priest of the Residence of Qa-a," *śm ḥ·t Nb·ty Q’-‘*, a fragment of the same in viii. 5.

Pl. x. 1—7. Cursive writing in ink: 1 perhaps shows the royal name [hieroglyph]; 3—5 may give various spellings of *Ḥms* or *Ḥms·t*, "Crocodile,"

as a proper name, later *Msḥ*. Cf. SETHE, *Verbum*, i., p. 151; *Dendereh*, Beb, Pl. xxxvii.D., l. 592, [hieroglyphs]. In 4 it seems to be [hieroglyphs]. Here the name is spelt by the word-sign [hieroglyph] *ḥms* as well as the full alphabetic spelling, and probably the determinative [hieroglyph]; cf. 5. The form of the bolt [hieroglyph] is interesting.

34. The rest of the inscriptions in this plate and in Pls. xi., xii. will be best treated in the order of the clear hand-copies following.

Pl. xiii. 2 = x. 9. Horus name Zet between [hieroglyphs] and [hieroglyphs]. The last group consists of signs difficult to recognize; but the second seems only a variant of [hieroglyph] *śḥm*, and the last may be the amulet or the Meskhent symbol mentioned in *Hieroglyphs*, p. 60; *Ptahhetep* I., fig. 22.

3 = xi. 1. Horus name Zet, with other signs.

5 = x. 10.

The ebony and ivory tablets of [hieroglyph] on pls. xiv.—xvi. are very remarkable. The most complete example is No. 16, on pl. xv. They seem to have been rectangular, and generally engraved on one side only. In the most important instances the design was divided vertically into two halves; that on the right comprised scenes and inscriptions in several registers, bounded on the outer edge by the sign [hieroglyph] "year" or "flourish." The other half consists of an inscription with the signs irregularly arranged, including titles of the king and of his officers. If [hieroglyph] means year, it may suggest that these tablets were brief annals of a reign, the year being marked by the chief events and the names of the chief officials.

Right half.—In No. 12 this is narrow. The [hieroglyph] is clear in 16 and in 25. The top register in 16 shows the king seated under a canopy with stepped base, and again running forward or dancing, holding the [hieroglyph] and perhaps the paddle [hieroglyph]. As in later times the symbol [hieroglyph] accompanies this scene (*Hieroglyphs*, p. 64, fig. 36). It represents a ceremony in the worship of the gods, but it does not here appear in whose honour the ceremony was performed. In 25 we see a bolt in a corresponding situation, which may possibly stand for [hieroglyph], the bolt (?) of the god Min (*Hieroglyphs*, p. 38), though it corresponds to the common alphabetic [hieroglyph] in x. 4. Here, then the worship may have been directed to Min of Coptos. The figure under the canopy can hardly be intended for Osiris, as the running figure is turned away from it. In 12 there is a *sed* canopy in the top register, with its name [hieroglyphs] rudely engraved.

The second register is nearly alike in 16 and 17. We see first [hieroglyph] *wp*, "open (?)," then a semicircular sign which we may connect either with [hieroglyph] desert or foreign land, or with a fortification [hieroglyph]. For the latter interpretation compare the breached fortress on the slate of Narmer from Hieraconpolis. This sign, however, encloses [hieroglyphs], and these suggest *wp* ʿꜣ *n sm·wt n* [hieroglyphs] *mr·w*, "opening the gate of the foreign lands to those that desire." The following part is very unintelligible, especially as 17 shows the same signs as 16, but differently arranged. In 12 the second register presents quite a different subject with hawk and ibis figures. In 25 apparently there is a sacred hawk on a perch [hieroglyph].

The third row is seen in 16 and 18, though imperfect. In the former we see a row of birds and [hieroglyphs], with other signs above. In the latter is the same royal title, following [hieroglyphs], possibly *nb pw yw*. So perhaps we may read "The Master comes, the King of Upper and Lower Egypt Semty," and after a gap [hieroglyphs], perhaps *yṯ šp*ꜣ*·t m*ʿ*b*ꜣ, "having seized thirty nomes" or "territories." There is also a mountainous oval containing [hieroglyphs]; this reminds one of the [hieroglyphs] forts of the Sinaitic peninsula destroyed by Una's army (*Una*, l. 24).

In No. 16 there seems to have been a fourth register; in 18 also probably the third was not the last, to judge by the remains on the other half, where the lowest signs are imperfect. Apparently in most cases the tablets have completely lost their lower ends.

Left side. In No. 12 this is the broader half, and the signs upon it are large, as in No. 15. 16 must again serve as the type. First there is the royal Horus name [hieroglyphs], and then the name and title of the chancellor Hemaka, [hieroglyphs] in 16 and 17; in 11 and 19 there is instead the name [hieroglyphs] Ka-sa (title lost). This person probably held the same position as Hemaka under Den, but at an earlier period. His name recurs in xxi. 18, on sealings from the tomb of Merneit, the predecessor of Den according to Prof. Petrie; Hemaka's name recurs in xxv. 53—56, from the tomb of Den. In 11 and 16 we have [hieroglyphs] *yṯ yś·t Ḥr·w*, "who took the throne of Horus." In 16 (cf. 18), [hieroglyphs] with [hieroglyph] may read *ḥ*ʿ *Tḥn·w*, "Sheikh of the Libyans"; but there is also the oil called [hieroglyphs] "*hatet*-oil of the Libyans"; and, as J. H. Walker has suggested to me, [hieroglyphs] might represent the later [hieroglyphs] *Tny*, This, the capital of the nome in which Abydos lay. Further, on 16, 18 and 11 there seems to have been [hieroglyphs] 1000, and 200 cubits (?), [hieroglyph] signifying a length of 100 cubits: or "Incense-trees, 200 trees." In 11 we also see perhaps [hieroglyphs] *sp tp*, "first time." On 14—17 we have signs representing enclosures (Residences) or other buildings. On the extreme left we see in 16, and trace in 15—17 (cf. also 14), an enclosure containing the sign of a man pounding (?), or opening the door of a trap (?); above him are [hieroglyph] and an axe. This might possibly mean "governor of the quarry city of Het-nub," where alabaster was found. Below it is [hieroglyph] *Ḥ·t-stn*, "the Residence of the King of Upper Egypt." This was the name of a city of some importance, in the XVIIIth nome, and from the inscription of Piankhy it was clearly on the east bank of the Nile, probably a little north of the latitude of Oxyrhynchus. Its suggestive name and its occurrence here lead us to suppose that it was of great importance in very early times. In No. 11, at about the corresponding place occurs ⟨glyph⟩ *yry Nḫn*, a very common title later; it means "he who belongs to Nekhen," and Nekhen is the Egyptian name of Hieraconpolis, the importance of which at the beginning of Egyptian history is shown by Quibell's finds, and is implied by its mythological significance. Perhaps one may conjecture that while Abydos was the metropolis of the Ist Dynasty, Hieraconpolis was its southern capital, and *Ḥ·t-stn* its northern capital in Upper Egypt. Lower Egypt would doubtless have its own separate traditional capital, of which the name ⟨glyph⟩ (above p. 37) suggests a probable situation.

On 16 we further see ⟨glyph⟩, perhaps meaning "royal smith" or "axe-maker," and unintelligible groups ⟨glyph⟩. In 18 ⟨glyph⟩ (?) in the corresponding place are not to be interpreted at present.

Pl. xvi. 20 = x. 11. The royal name Semty, followed by an inscription the first part of which Professor Petrie conjectures to mean "the great chiefs come to the tomb": one might complete this translation with the words, "that he may give them ⟨glyph⟩, the reward of long service." But this is more than doubtful. l would at this period have a definite numerical significance; ⟨glyph⟩ for ⟨glyph⟩ is possible, but not likely; and ⟨glyph⟩ for "give" is very rare, even later. Professor Petrie's rendering of the first words is very plausible. The repetition of signs three times for the plural is interesting, though to be expected for this period, and recurs in x. 9. The sign which is compared by Prof. Petrie to the plan of a tomb is allied to the sign for ⟨glyph⟩ (*Pyr. M.* 15 = *P.* 12), sometimes meaning "the two (?) aisles" of an audience chamber, and to the determinative of *Pr-wr*, "Great House" or "Great Chamber," and other words in the texts of the Pyramids.

Pl. xvi. 21 = xi. 11, like the last, is well engraved and noteworthy. We recognise upon it a good instance of a form of □ that is common on the monuments of the Ist Dynasty. The typical form is mat-like, but it has been hitherto open to more than one interpretation. Here it is seen to consist of crossed fibres, without any edging or hard outline. Evidently it is here no packet, or stool, nor even a finished mat, but simply represents platting or mat-work. This corroborates the suggestion in *Hieroglyphs*, pp. 3, 47, that □ represents pictorially the name of a city called *P* as being the city of Matwork, and so obtained its alphabetic value *p* (cf. the probable history of ⟨glyph⟩ = *Nḫb, Hieroglyphs*, p. 29). Following the □ there may be ⟨glyph⟩, and the signs representing the last two joints of a finger with the nail, and perhaps intended for ⟨glyph⟩ *ʿn·t*, "nail," "claw," unless it be *zbʿ*, "finger," "10,000."

Pl. xvi. 22. With ⟨glyph⟩. Cf. xvii. 26, 29.

Pl. xvii. 26 = xii. 1. This is a perfect tablet of the type of those just dealt with (xv. 16, &c.). On the right half, which is bounded by the large ⟨glyph⟩ sign, is a boat on water, and above it the legend ⟨glyph⟩ *šmś-Ḥrw*, "follower of Horus"; another boat is at the base, containing a bird. Above it is a figure of an ape seated on a stool, probably representing Thoth, and perhaps ⟨glyph⟩ "palace of the great ones." On the other half are the dual kingdom and Nebty titles, followed by the name which seems to correspond to Semempses in Manetho and to ⟨glyph⟩ in Sety's list. Here the man wears a wig, and appears to be wrapped in a long cloth wound round the body, with the end projecting in front of his waist. The figure bears a curious resemblance to some late linear forms of the sign ⟨glyph⟩ *šmś*, "follow," as written in many texts, but this may be only accidental, the example of the simple form ⟨glyph⟩ on this tablet being very different. It has been suggested that the sign in Sety's list (recurring in MAR., *Mast.*, 198) represents a *sm* priest of Ptah, *sm-n-Ptḥ*, and so Σεμεμψης; but the regular dress of the *sem*-priest is very different from the dress of that figure and of its earlier prototype (*B.H.* IV., pl. xiv. and p. 3).

Beyond the royal titles are ⟨hieroglyphs⟩. Possibly we may render this, "He who traverses the Pool of Horus (cf. 28), the royal axe-maker (cf. xv. 16), the first, the governor Henu-ka (cf. 28)." Three more characters follow, but are obscure.

27. Part of *stn·y by·ty* and Nebty titles, as Maspero suggests.

28 = xi. 12. The injured compartment on the right would seem to give a king's name Ket . . , Ket-ur (?). To make ⟨hieroglyph⟩ (?) the determinative of ⟨hieroglyph⟩ would be against the concise spelling of kings' names. The rest of the signs on the tablet are uninjured: ⟨hieroglyphs⟩ make an obscure combination, cf. 26 and xv. 16.

29 corresponds to some extent with 26, having on the right the ⟨sign⟩, the boat with throne, and ⟨signs⟩ above. On left, Horus name Qa-a, with a special Nebty name ⟨sign⟩ Sen, not found elsewhere. Beyond is ⟨hieroglyphs⟩ (?) "Doing things, distinguishing (?), royal axe-maker (?)."

30. The word designating the captive seems to be ⟨hieroglyph⟩ i.e. *Sty*, "the Asiatic (?)," followed by an oval sign of land.

35. We now reach the long series of jar sealings rolled from cylinders (cf. xii. 3—7), which Prof. Petrie has so carefully copied from numerous impressions, each more or less imperfect and obscure.

Pl. xviii. 1. The Horus name of Zet.

2, 3. The same with ⟨hieroglyphs⟩ *Yty*, meaning "Reigning Sovereign," perhaps his personal name Aty, in Sety's list ⟨hieroglyphs⟩.

4. The same with ⟨hieroglyphs⟩ *R-ʿwy*, "entrance of two doors," which may have reference to the frontier stations, alternating with the figure of an embattled enclosure containing the characters ⟨hieroglyphs⟩.

5. The same enclosure, alternating with ⟨hieroglyphs⟩. Probably ⟨hieroglyphs⟩, recurring in xxiii. 40 with the name Hetep, is a title, *śzty* (?), "sealer (?)," and the other two signs form a proper name.

6. The same name and title with another title ⟨hieroglyph⟩ *ʿd mr*, common in later times; a city name, possibly ⟨hieroglyphs⟩ *Db*; a sign resembling a man swimming. Cf. perhaps 81 on pl. xxix.

Pl. xix. 7. Same name and title with ⟨hieroglyphs⟩ *ymwt*, ⟨hieroglyph⟩ and ⟨hieroglyphs⟩ "inheritance of the original god (?)."

8. ⟨hieroglyphs⟩ and other signs.

9. ⟨hieroglyphs⟩ and birds. The sign ⟨sign⟩ recurs of the same form in xxv. 50, &c.

10. ⟨hieroglyphs⟩ (the ⟨sign⟩ holds a curved wand in one hand), "Chief of the three dancers (?)" (compare *Deshasheh*, pl. xii. and p. 47 note), or "Chief of the three throwers of the boomerang (?)."

11. A very remarkable example of cursive accounts. At the top is probably a date ⟨hieroglyphs⟩ "10th day, festival of . . . ." Then follow names of articles indicated by vague picture-signs, with numerals beneath, ⟨hieroglyphs⟩ "20," ⟨hieroglyphs⟩ "220." This was no doubt intelligible enough as a reminder to the scribe, but to us it is very obscure.

12 includes the boomerang-thrower, a bird resembling an ostrich, and a group of ⟨sign⟩ and ⟨sign⟩ which often occurs on private stelae of this period (pls. xxxi., xxxii.). It may read *kʾ yʾḥ*, "spiritualized *ka*," as a term for a deceased person in a state of bliss; or it may be a priestly title such as *s·yʾḥ kʾ* (?), "he who spiritualizes the *ka*," by services.

15. The same group with ⟨hieroglyph⟩ and ⟨hieroglyph⟩ *Ḥ·t yḥ·t* (?), "Residence of the cow (?)," which if rightly read is the name of a city in the Western Delta (Libyan nome), or perhaps of some other city such as Dendereh, which was dedicated to the cow-goddess Hathor.

16. The "glorified *ka* (?), Ap."

18. Strange swimming signs, &c., and ⟨sign⟩ "overseer."

20. ⟨hieroglyphs⟩ (?) in mountainous oval, and other signs.

Pl. xxi. 24, 25. Titles with the name (?) ⸢𓂋𓅃𓎛⸣.

26. The Horus name Den and ⸢𓈖 𓋹⸣ (?).

27. 𓋹 ⸢𓏏𓏤⸣ "overseer, the middle," cf. xxiv. 44, &c. In the sign of the heart its vessels are shown much more prominently at this time than later.

28. The name ⸢𓎡𓏤⸣ Ka-sa, cf. xvi. 19, accompanied by a title ⸢𓂝𓁹⸣ (?), "eyes of the king (?)."

29. The name (?) ⸢𓆛⸣ Ath, accompanied by ⸢𓋹𓎡⸣ (?), Ankh-ka, perhaps a city name: the last sign, which occurs so commonly in these groups, may be ⸢𓏏⸣, perhaps as a word-sign. Two vases in a rectangle, with ⸢𓎛�⸣ hz sometimes inside, sometimes outside, reading *Pr-hz* . . . . ; cf. note to 35.

30. The same name with ⸢𓊪𓎡⸣ Śenb-ka (?), ⸢𓎾⸣ and ⸢𓃀⸣ (?).

31. Here we may perhaps recognise a vine-trellis, with other signs.

34. ⸢𓋹𓏤⸣ "the Councillor," followed by ⸢𓐍𓃹⸣ Chnem.

35. ⸢𓋹𓏏⸣ in a rectangle ⸢▢⸣ is evidently the same as ⸢𓋹𓏏⸣ *ḥry-ʿ pr-ḥz*, "assistant in the treasury," xxiii. 40.

Pl. xxiii. 37. Possibly "wine-press of the East in the nomes of the North," and, 38, "wine-press of the West in the nomes of the North."

39. "Treasurer of the King of Lower Egypt in the store (*mḫr*?) of the Saite nome." For the importance of the Saite nome at this period, see the note to pl. i.

40. "The assistant in the treasury, the Sezty-sealer (?) Hetep."

41. The "Sezty Hetep" and unknown signs.

42. "Chnemhetep (?)."

43. ⸢𓊃𓎼𓎡⸣ and other signs.

Pl. xxiv. 44. Cf. 45, xxi. 27, and xxv. 50.

45. ⸢𓅅𓏤𓏠𓎡⸣ "promoting the rock of Horus (?)," in a mountainous oval.

Pl. xxv. 53—56. Interesting as containing clearly the name ⸢𓋹𓊃𓎡⸣, with titles found scattered on other sealings, viz., the well-known ⸢𓆛𓏤⸣ and ⸢𓋹⸣ (53) ; ⸢𓅅𓋹⸣ in a mountainous oval, probably as the name of a city or country ; ⸢𓋹𓏏𓏤⸣ 55, cf. 27, 44, 50 ; ⸢𓋹𓎡⸣ (?) or ⸢𓋹𓌉⸣ 54, cf. 47, &c., 63, 64, 83, 84 ; and two kinds of vases together, cf. 47.

Pl. xxvi. 58. The two-kingdom title with name of Merpaba, followed by ⸢▢⸣ containing the same title with Her-pa-ua (?), as in the inscriptions of Qa-a, ix. 3, &c., and ⸢𓅃𓋹𓎛⸣, i.e., probably *ḥʾt*, "tomb." The one-barbed hook or harpoon-head, possibly *wʿ*, "one" (*Hieroglyphs*, p. 52), or *dś*, "blade" (*ib.*, p. 50, L. D., ii. 13), is similar to that which is figured in the talons of a hawk in the palette of Narmer. Perhaps Her-pa-ua is the name of the sepulchral city or tomb of Merpaba.

Pl. xxvii. 64—67. Titles of ⸢𓋹𓂋𓃀⸣ *Sʿb*, Sabu, who was ⸢𓆛𓏤⸣, ⸢𓋹𓌉⸣ (?), ⸢𓅅𓏤⸣ in a mountainous oval, &c., cf. 81, &c.

68 contains a title connected with the "royal vineyard (?)."

Pl. xxviii. 77 has several well-defined and remarkable signs, difficult to identify.

Pl. xxix. 85, a remarkable little seal, difficult to interpret.

36. Pl. xxx. The important stela figured in this plate (= xxxvi. 48) shows the figure of a noble standing, holding staff and ⸢𓋹⸣, in the attitude commonly seen in tomb sculptures. His name ⸢𓋹𓂋𓆑⸣ *Sʾb-f*, Sabef, is behind him in large characters. Above, in smaller writing, are his titles. The first is probably expressed by the ⸢▢⸣ containing ⸢𓈖𓅅𓂋⸣ "the governor of the Residence (*ḥʾty*?) of 'All Protection behind,'" which Prof. Petrie (above, p. 21) considers to be the name of the tomb of Qa-a. We then have ⸢𓋹𓏏𓏤⸣ "regulator of the festival" or "tent," a well-known title in Old Kingdom tombs for a person connected perhaps with the tomb service. After this comes ⸢𓏏𓏤⸣ *ḫnt* and ⸢𓅅𓏤⸣ *Hʾty* (?) *wʿ* (?) *pw . rʾw*, believed by Prof. Petrie to be the name of the palace. Next comes ⬜ 𓏏𓏤 *šmr pr-stn*, "friend in the palace" (cf. xxxi. 40), 𓃢 𓏏 *ḥry šštˀ (n) wꜣ·t mdw*, "over the secrets of decrees," and further 𓃥 𓏏 (P) 𓉐 " priest of (?) Anubis in the Divine Abode (?)." The title of Anubis with the feathers on the animal occurs very similarly in the ancient tomb of Kha-bau-Seker at Saqqareh, MAR., *Mast.*, p. 77; cf. above, xxix. 86. The remaining titles and signs at the left hand end are obscure.

This stela belongs to the end of the Ist Dynasty, and is the most highly developed of those found. A comparison with the panels of Hesy and the tomb of Kha-bau-Seker shows what great progress took place in the art of design and sculpture between the end of the Ist Dynasty and the end of the IIIrd Dynasty, which is the latest period to which these two monuments can possibly be attributed.

The inscriptions from stelae, sealings, &c., on pls. xxxi., xxxii. present many interesting points for further investigation, but time does not admit of a full examination of them here. We note curious names, strange signs, difficult titles, and perhaps some determinative signs.

The above hasty remarks on these most interesting remains of a remote past, it is to be hoped, will quickly be rendered nugatory by further investigation in the study and further discovery in the field.

INDEX.

LONDON
PRINTED BY GILBERT AND RIVINGTON, LTD.
ST. JOHN'S HOUSE, CLERKENWELL.

1.   VIEW FROM KOM ES SULTAN. ROYAL CEMETERY IN FAR DISTANCE.

2.   VIEW FROM FORT (SHUNEH). ROYAL CEMETERY IN DISTANCE.

3.   ROYAL CEMETERY FROM HEQRESHU HILL.

4.   ROYAL CEMETERY. WALL OF TOMB OF ZER IN FOREGROUND.

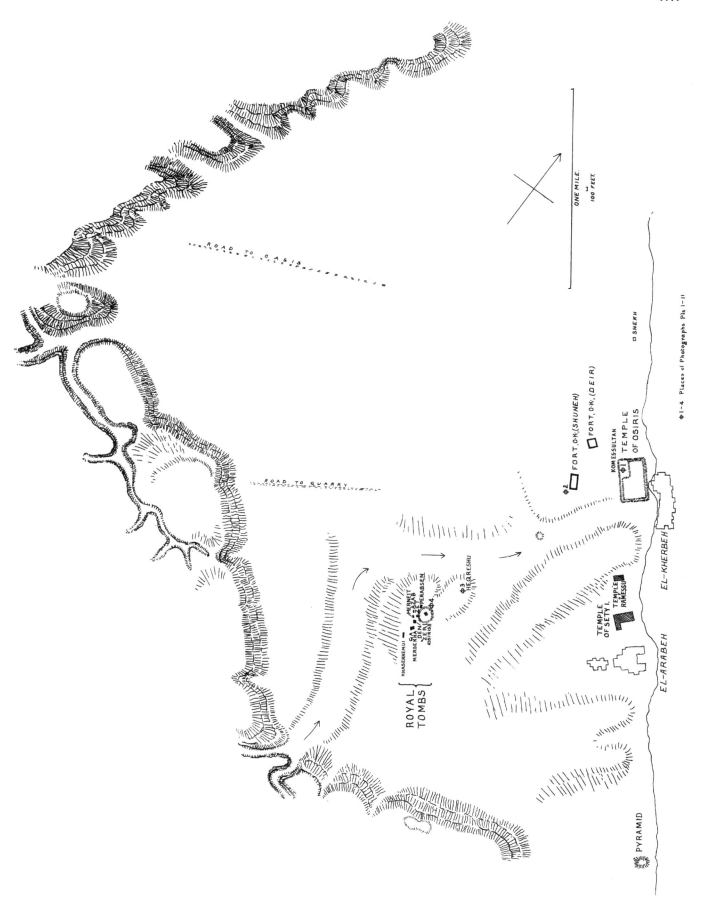

ONE MILE
100 FEET

ROAD TO OASIS

ROAD TO QUARRY

FORT. O.K. (SHUNEH)

FORT. O.K. (DEIR)

Φ2

KOM ESSULTAN

TEMPLE OF OSIRIS

Φ1

☐ SHEKH

Φ1-4 Places of Photographs Pls 1-11

Φ3 HEQRESHU

Φ4.

KHASEKHEMUI
MERNEIT
QA
DEN
MERSEKHA
ZER
PERABSEN
AZAB
(OSIRIS)

ROYAL TOMBS

TEMPLE OF SETY I.

TEMPLE RAMESSU

EL-KHERBEH

EL-ARABEH

PYRAMID

1. AHA—MENA.   CRYSTAL.
Bought.

2. NARMER.   ALABASTER.
Tomb of Zet.

3. ZESER.   METAMORPHIC.
Tomb of Zet.
(IVORY. *Tomb of Den.*)

4. ZET.   SERPENTINE.
Tomb Z.3.

5.   VOLCANIC ASH.
Tomb of Zet.

6.   ALABASTER.
Tomb W.34.

7.   CRYSTAL.
Tomb of Merneit.

8.   ALABASTER.
Tomb of Merneit.

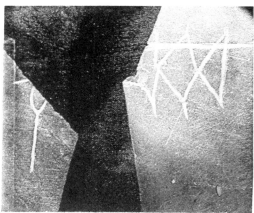

9. SLATE.   10.   SLATE.
Tomb of Merneit.

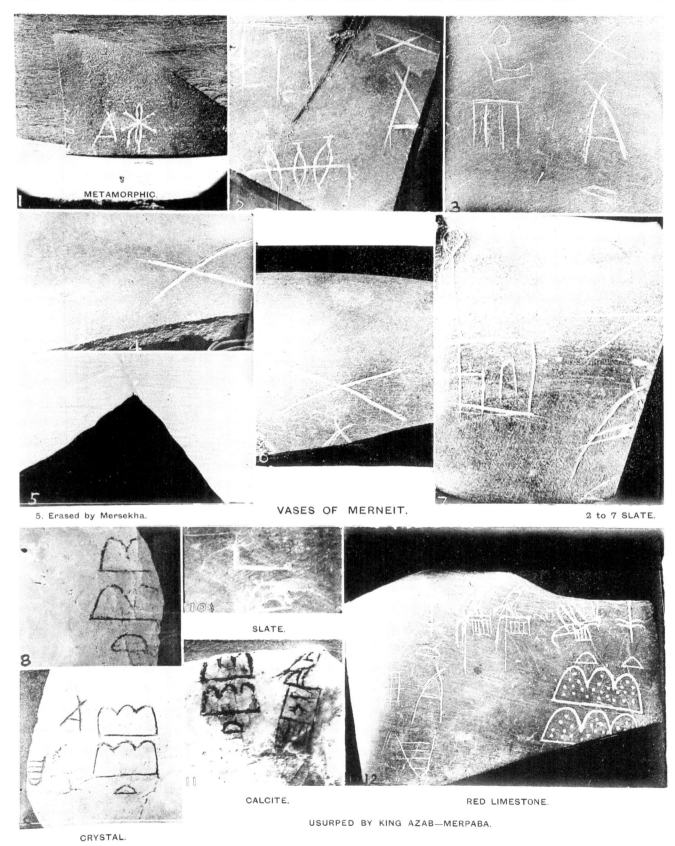

METAMORPHIC.

5. Erased by Mersekha.   VASES OF MERNEIT.   2 to 7 SLATE.

SLATE.

CALCITE.   RED LIMESTONE.

USURPED BY KING AZAB—MERPABA.

CRYSTAL.

VASES OF DEN—SETUI.

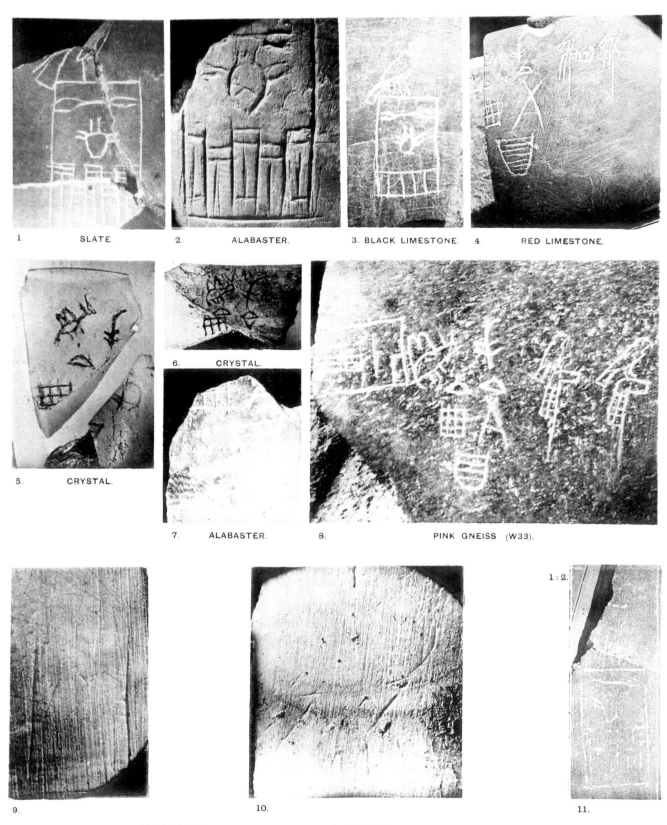

1.   SLATE.   2.   ALABASTER.   3. BLACK LIMESTONE.   4   RED LIMESTONE.

5.   CRYSTAL.   6.   CRYSTAL.

7.   ALABASTER.   8.   PINK GNEISS (W33).

1:2.

9.   10.   11.

ALABASTER JARS, ERASED, FROM TOMB OF KING MERSEKHA.

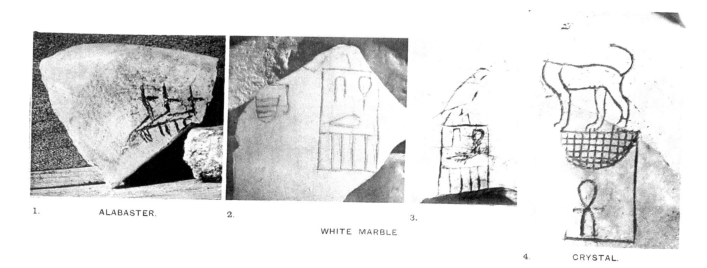

1.   ALABASTER.   2.   3.

WHITE MARBLE.

4.   CRYSTAL.

6.   CRYSTAL.

9.   POTTERY.

5.   ALABASTER.   7.   8.

CRYSTAL.

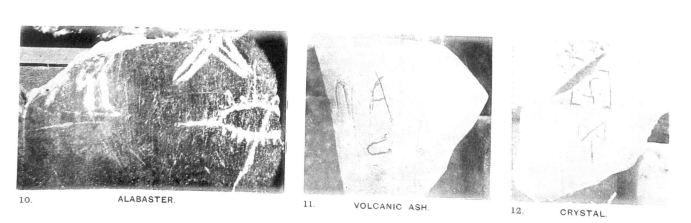

10.   ALABASTER.   11.   VOLCANIC ASH.   12.   CRYSTAL.

1. WHITE MARBLE.   2. WHITE MARBLE.   3. WHITE MARBLE.   4. WHITE MARBLE.   VOLCANIC ASH. 5.

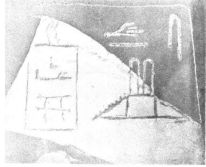

7.   WHITE MARBLE.   8.   WHITE MARBLE.   7a joins No. 7.

6.   VOLCANIC ASH.

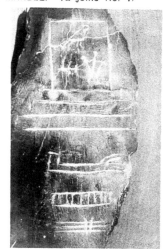

9.   WHITE MARBLE.   10.   WHITE MARBLE.   11.   ALABASTER 1:2.

12.   GREY MARBLE.   13.   GREY MARBLE.   14.   GREY MARBLE.

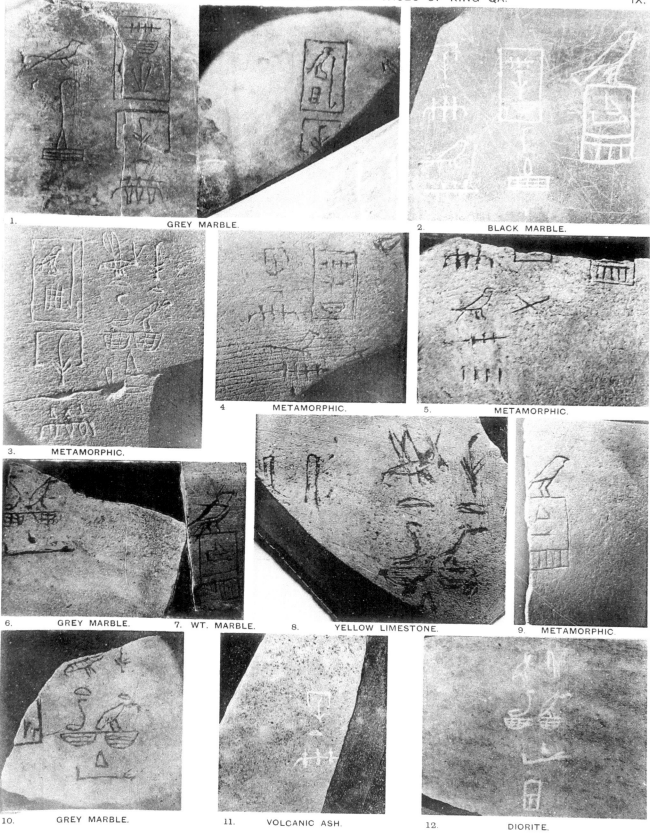

1. GREY MARBLE. 2. BLACK MARBLE.

3. METAMORPHIC. 4 METAMORPHIC. 5. METAMORPHIC.

6. GREY MARBLE. 7. WT. MARBLE. 8. YELLOW LIMESTONE. 9. METAMORPHIC.

10. GREY MARBLE. 11. VOLCANIC ASH. 12. DIORITE.

1. SETUI SLATE.   2. SLATE. Mersekha.   3.   SLATE. Mersekha Tomb.   4.   ALABASTER. Qa Tomb.

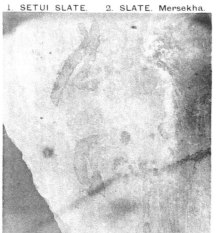

8   ZET. IVORY.

5.   ALABASTER. Qa Tomb.   6, 7.   ALABASTER. Qa Tomb

9.   ZET. IVORY BOX.   10.   ZET. Tomb Z 3.   11.   DEN. IVORY.

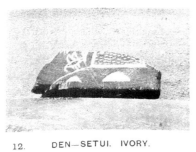

12.   DEN—SETUI. IVORY.   13.   DEN—SETUI IVORY, AND REVERSE.   14. DEN—SETUI. IVORY.

4:3.

ABYDOS. IVORY AND EBONY TABLETS OF KINGS ZET, DEN, &c.

XI.

1, 2. ZET.

3—7. DEN.

8—11. DEN.

12. Tomb of Qa.

13 Tomb of Azab.

14—16. DEN.

17. Tomb of Den.

18. Tomb of Mersekha.

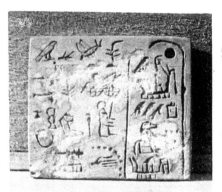

1. KING SEMEMPSES. IVORY. 4 3.
From his Tomb.

2. KING QA. IVORY. 4 : 3.
From his Tomb.

3. JAR SEALING. Tomb of King Merneit.

4. KING DEN. JAR SEALING.

5. KING QA. JAR SEALINGS. From his Tomb.   6.

7. KING DEN. SEALING. 4 : 3.

8. IVORY LEGS OF CASKETS. 2 : 3.   9.

12. 1 : 3.

13.   5 : 4.
GAMING REED. IVORY.
Tomb of King Qa.

10. RELIEF IN VEINED MARBLE.
Tomb of Zet.

11.   COPPER BOWL.   1 : 3.
Tomb of Mersekha.

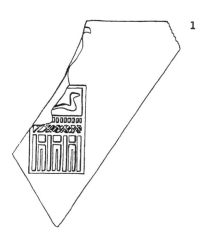

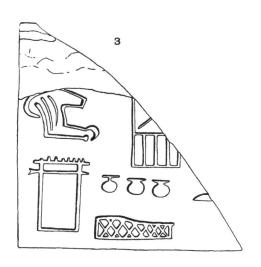

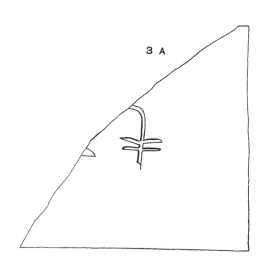

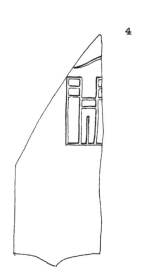

Z 3

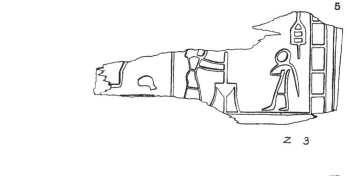

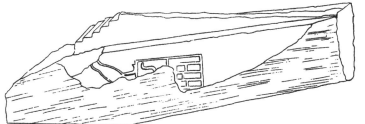

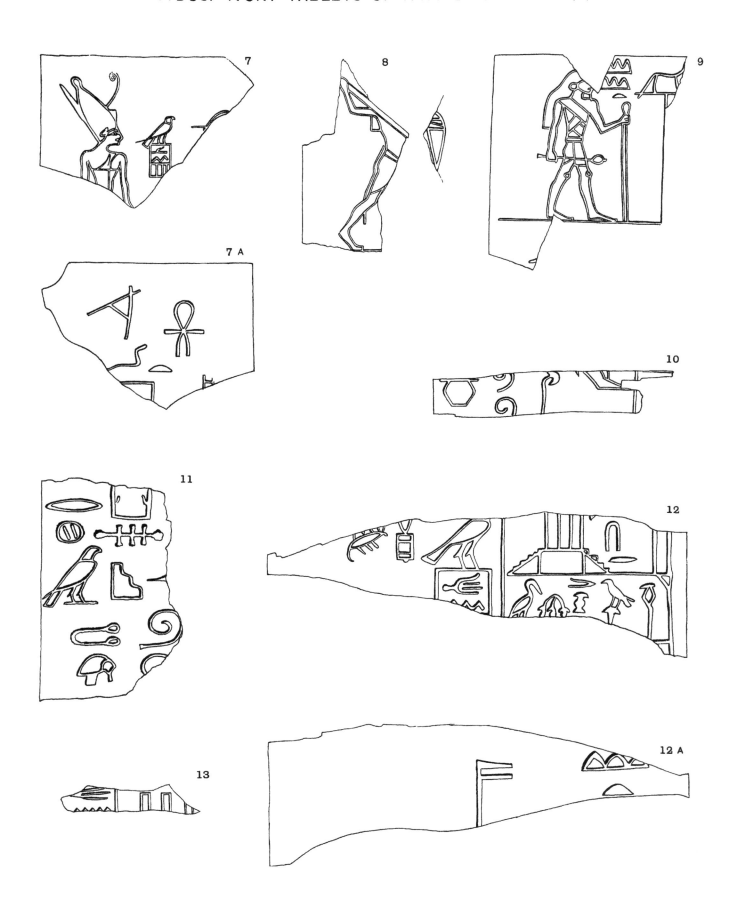

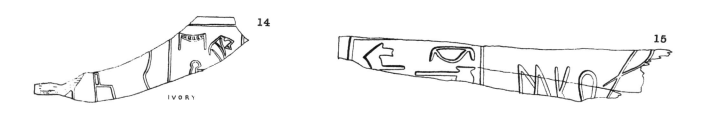

14

15

IVORY

16

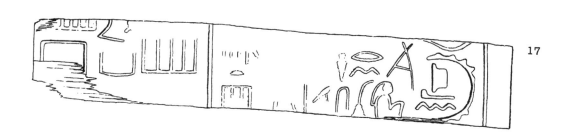

17

18

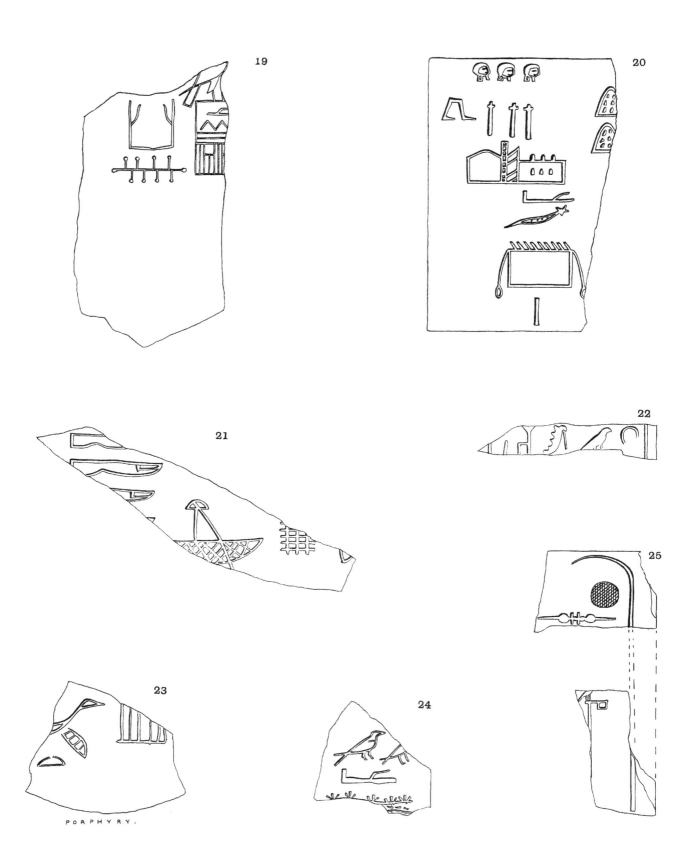

PORPHYRY.

26

U

27

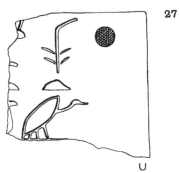

U

28

Q

29

Q

1 : 1   30

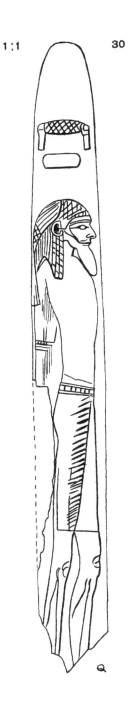

Q

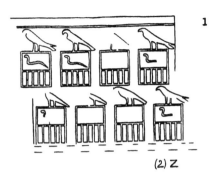

(2) Z

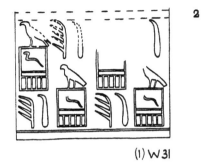

(1) W 31

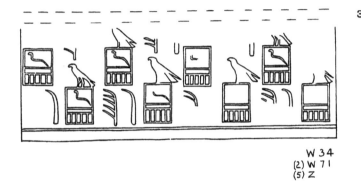

W 34
(2) W 71
(5) Z

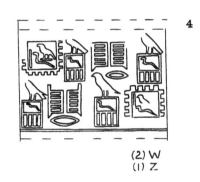

(2) W
(1) Z

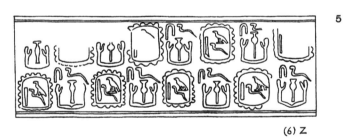

(6) Z

(2) Z

7

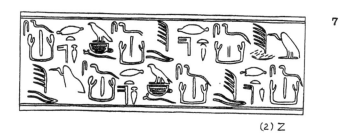

(2) Z

8

(8) Z

9

(3) Z

10

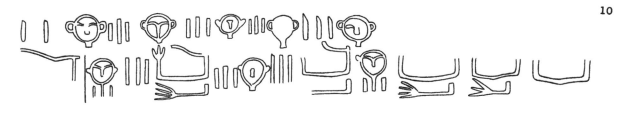

(1) T.
(5) Z

11

On base of dish.
Z

12

13

14

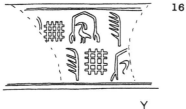

15

16

17

Y

18

19

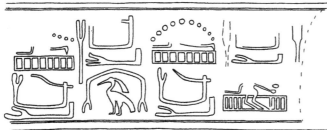

20

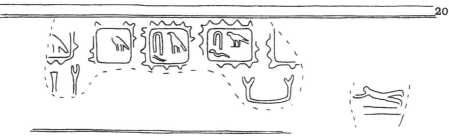

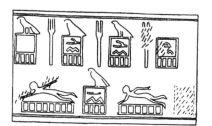

21

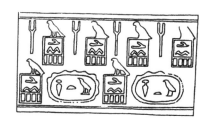

22

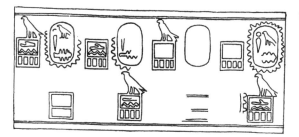

23

24

25

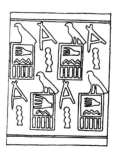

26

·Y 32

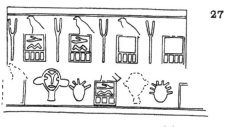

27

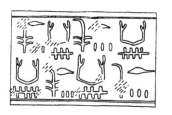

28

(4)

Y 22

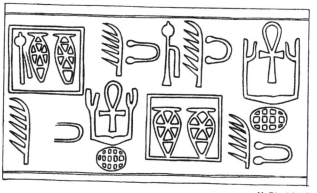

29

X 51. Y 26

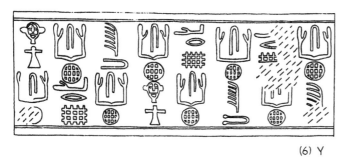

30

(6) Y

31

Y

32

Y

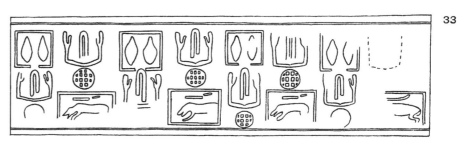

33

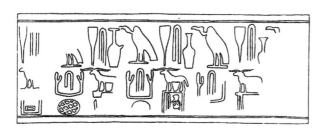

34

35

Y. 26

36

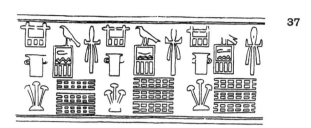

37

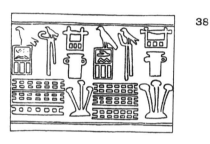

38

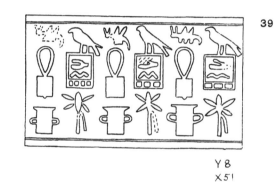

39

Y 8
X 5¹

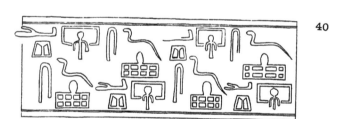

40

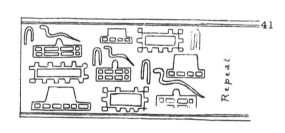

41

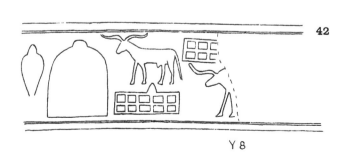

42

Y 8

43

Y 6

44

45

T

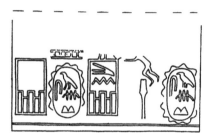

46

47

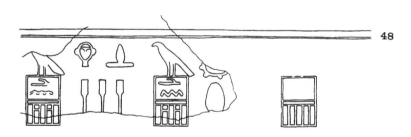

48

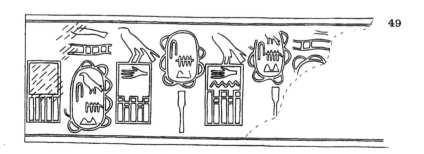

49

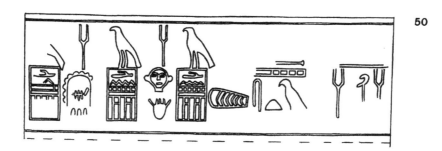

50

51

52

53

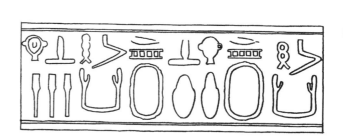

54

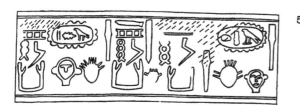

55

56

(8) T

57

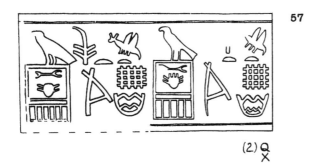

(2) Q
X

58

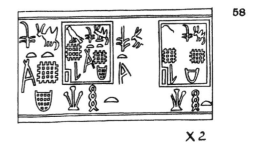

X 2

59

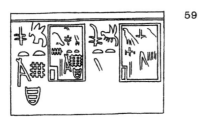

60

X 2

61

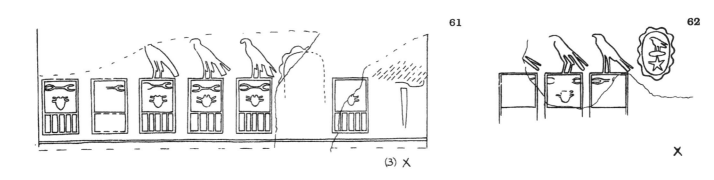

(3) X

62

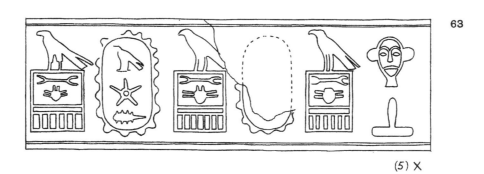

X

63

(5) X

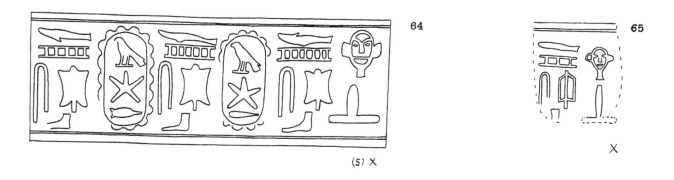

64

65

(5) X

X

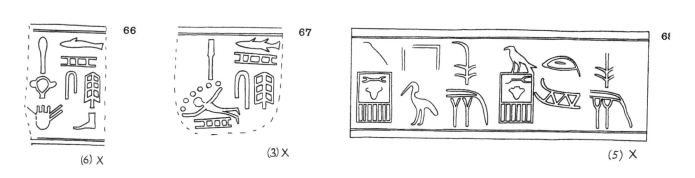

66

67

68

(6) X

(3) X

(5) X

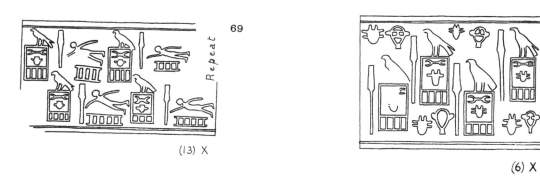

69

70

Repeat

(13) X

(6) X

2:1

71

X.2

4:3

72

73

74

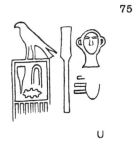

75

U

76

U

77

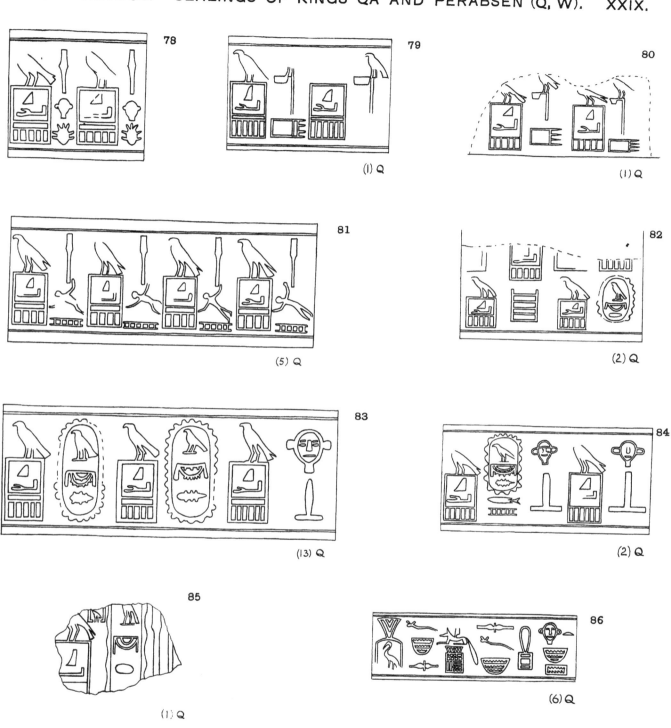

78

79

(1) Q

80

(1) Q

81

(5) Q

82

(2) Q

83

(13) Q

84

(2) Q

85

(1) Q

86

(6) Q

87

(2) W 30

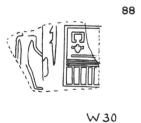

88

W 30

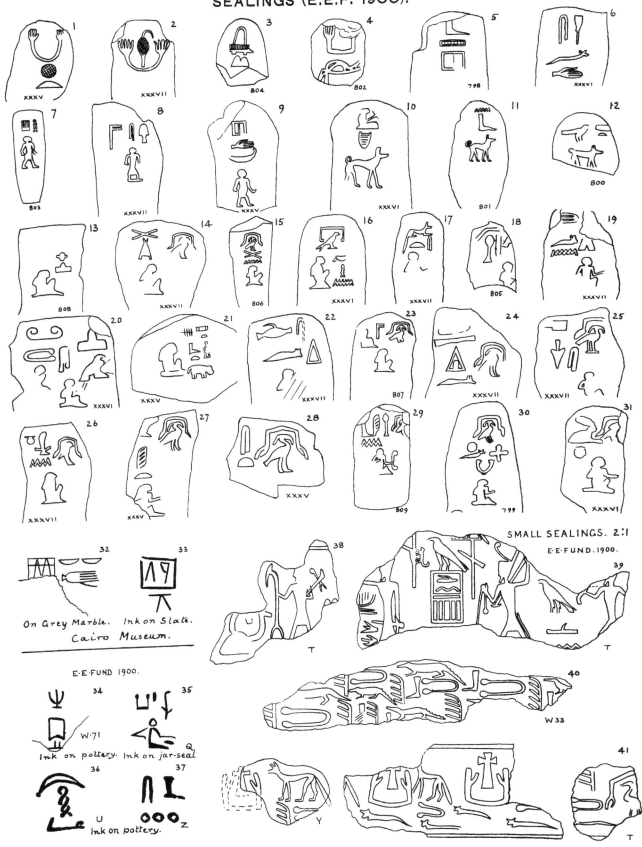

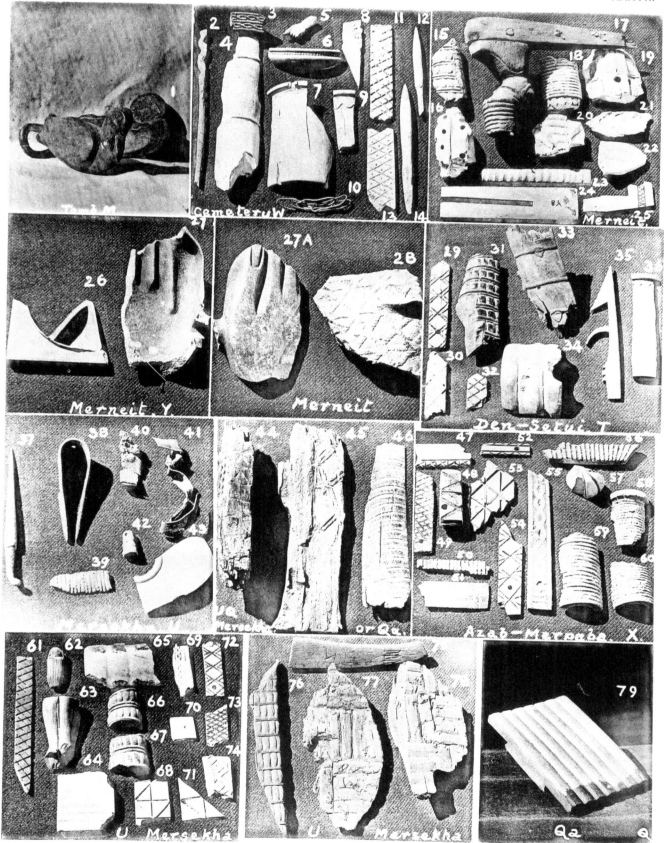

Tomb M   Cemetery W   Merneit

27

26   Merneit. Y   27A   28   Merneit

Den-Serui. T

U   Merneit   or Qa   Azab-Merpaba. X

U Mersekha   U Mersekha   Qa   Q

ABYDOS.   STONE VASES AND POTTERY, 1st DYNASTY.   JAMB OF HA-AB-RA.   XXXVIII.

1. HARD MARBLE VASE. 4 : 3   2.   CRYSTAL VASE.   4 : 3   3. MODEL WATERSKIN IN MARBLE. U. 1 : 2

4. ALABASTER VASE BASE. 1 : 2   5.   MODEL VASES OF PAINTED LIMESTONE.   From Tomb Q 20.   6.

7.   MERNEIT, UNDISTURBED CHAMBER. Y 2.

8. ALABASTER JAR AND BOWL, SLATE BOWL. Q 21. 1 : 5

9.   POTTERY, AMORITE STYLE.   10.   DOOR JAMB OF HA-AB-RA (APRIES) XXVI. DYN., FROM CENOTAPH OF OSIRIS.   11

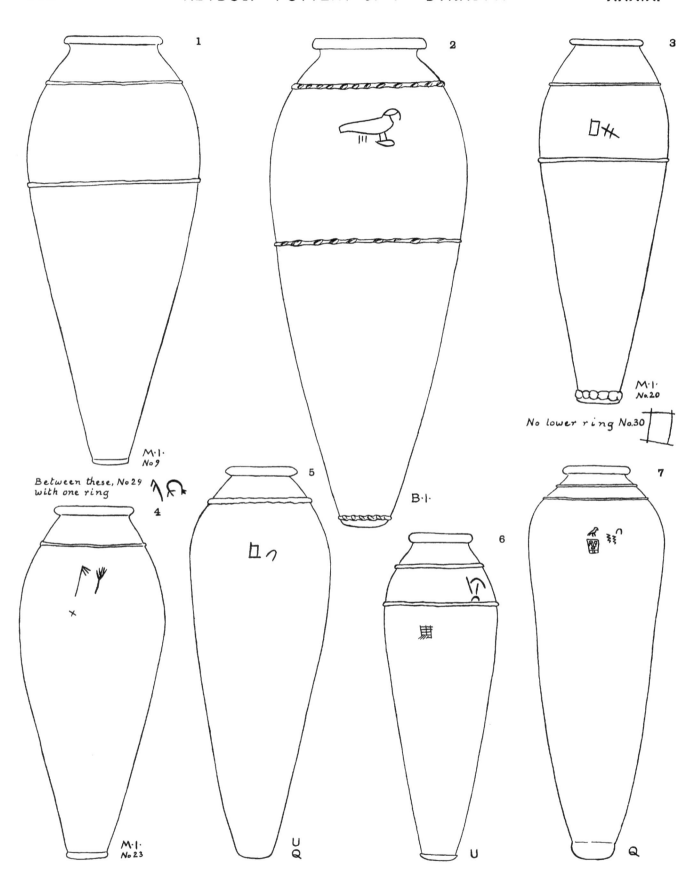

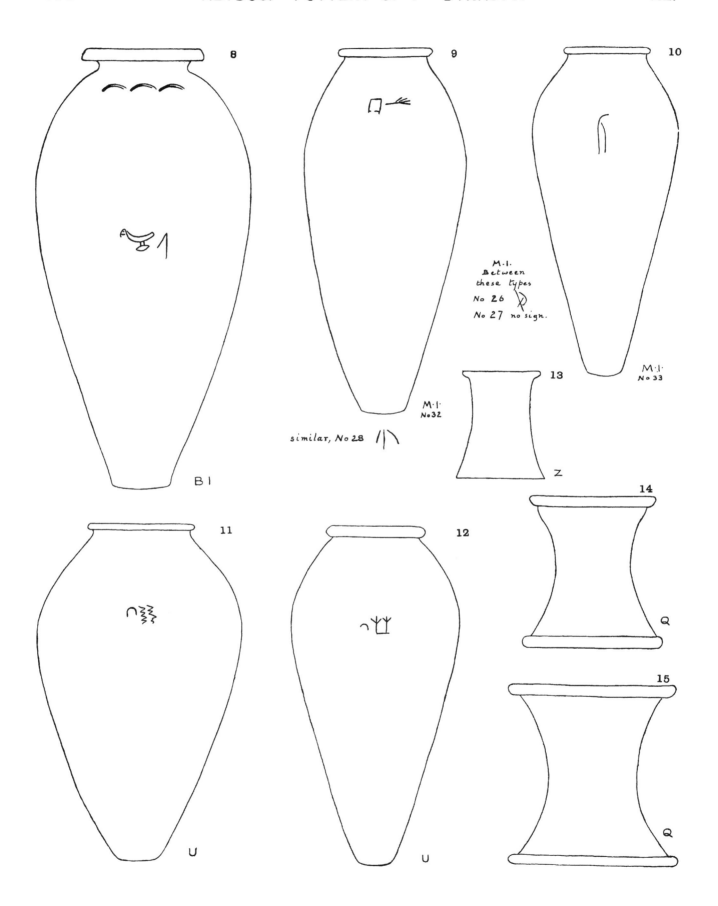

8

B I

9

similar, No 28

M·I·
No32

10

M·I·
Between
these types
No 26
No 27 no sign.

13

Z

M·I·
No 33

11

U

12

U

14

Q

15

Q

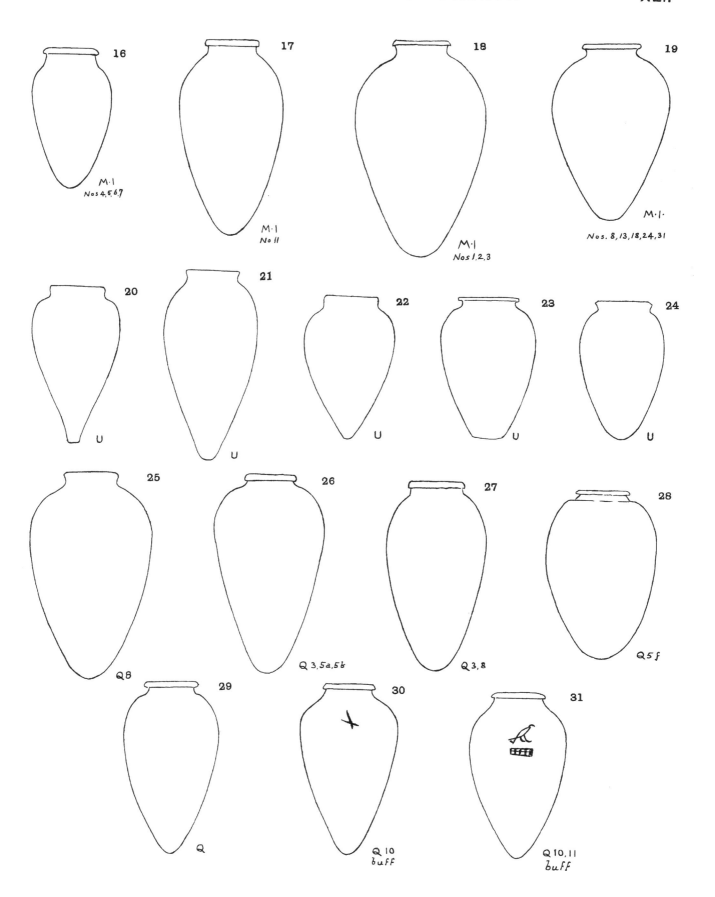

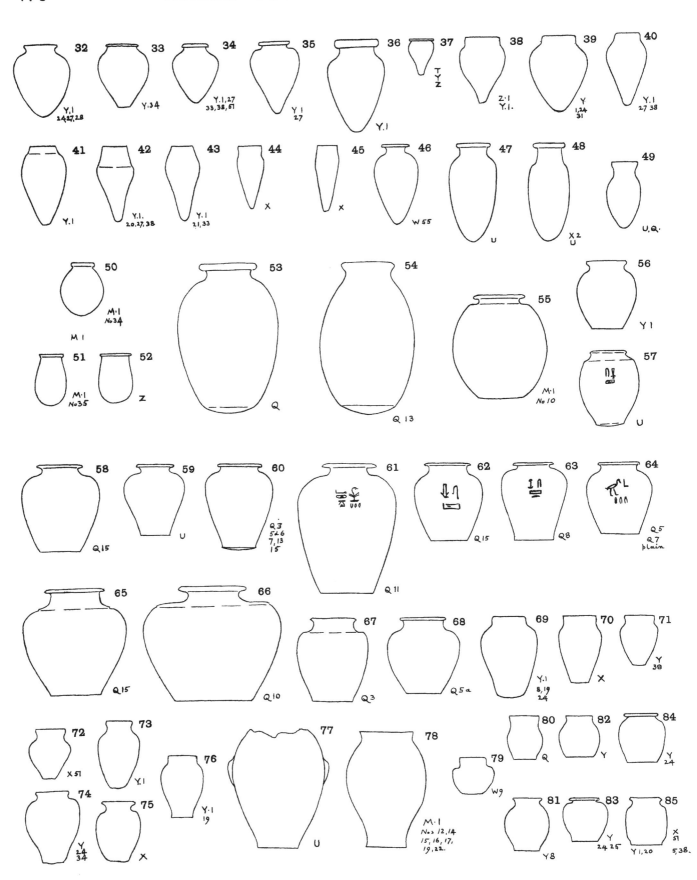

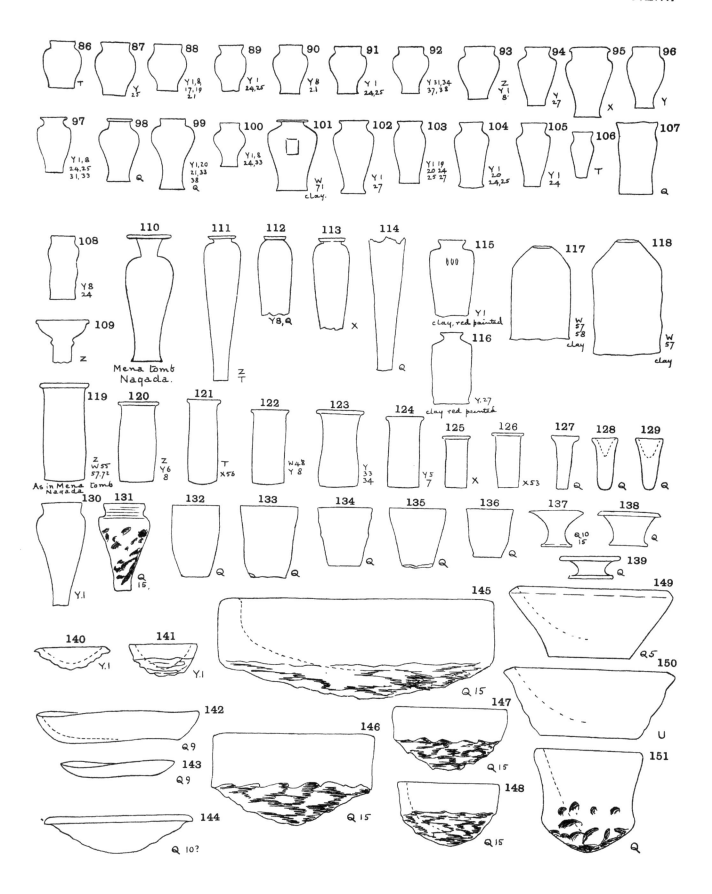

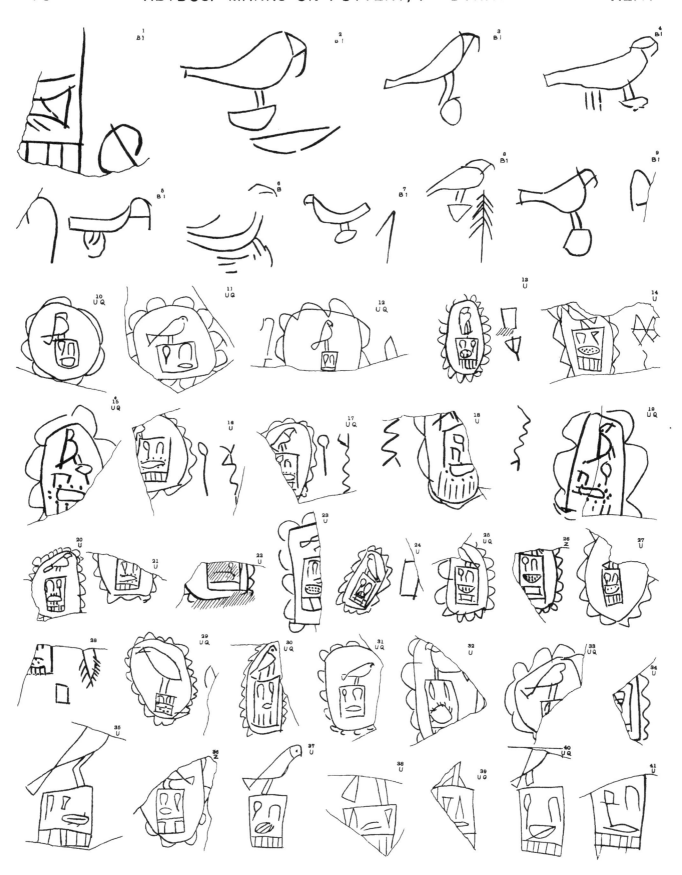

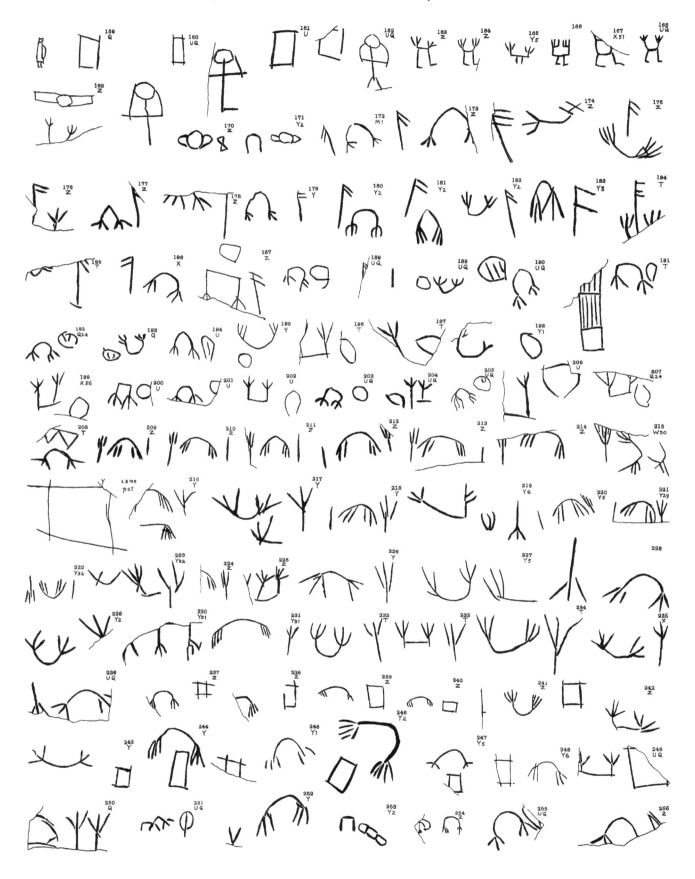

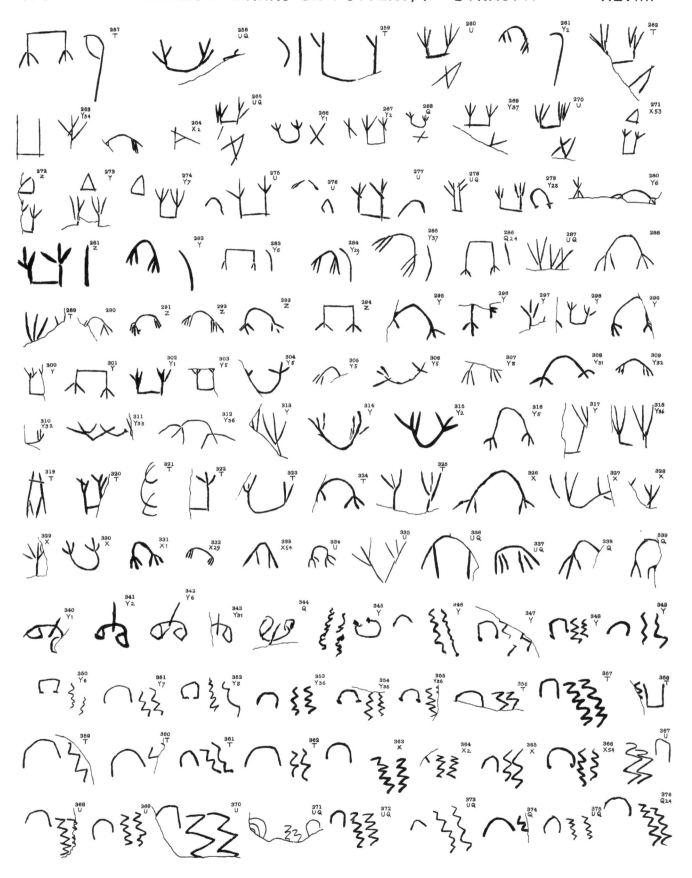

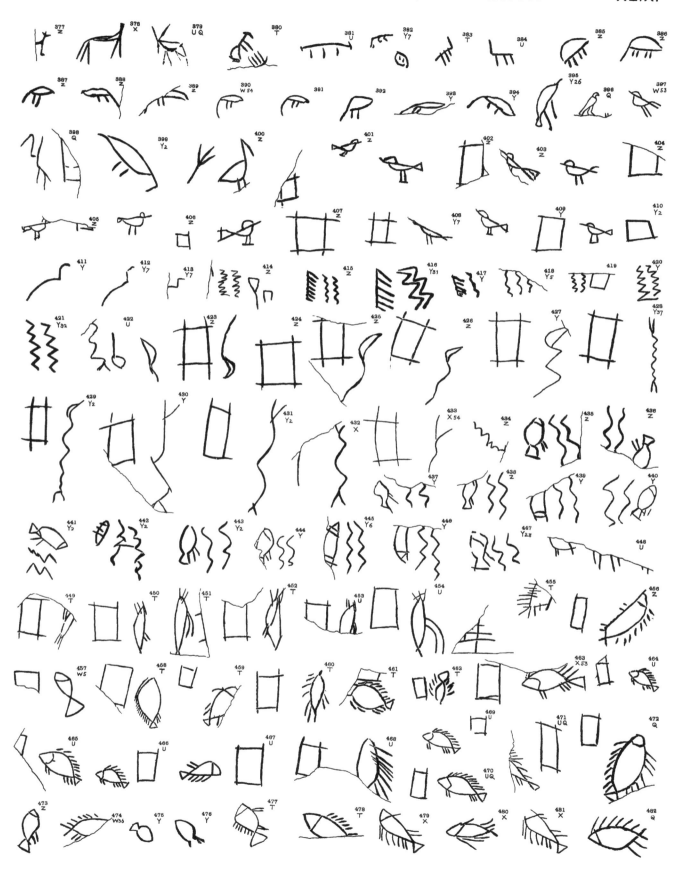

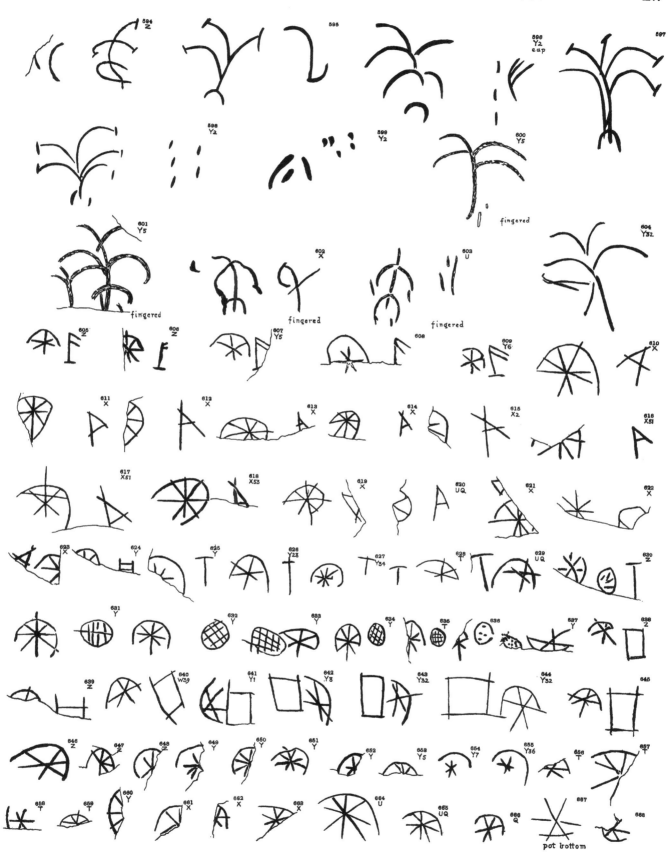

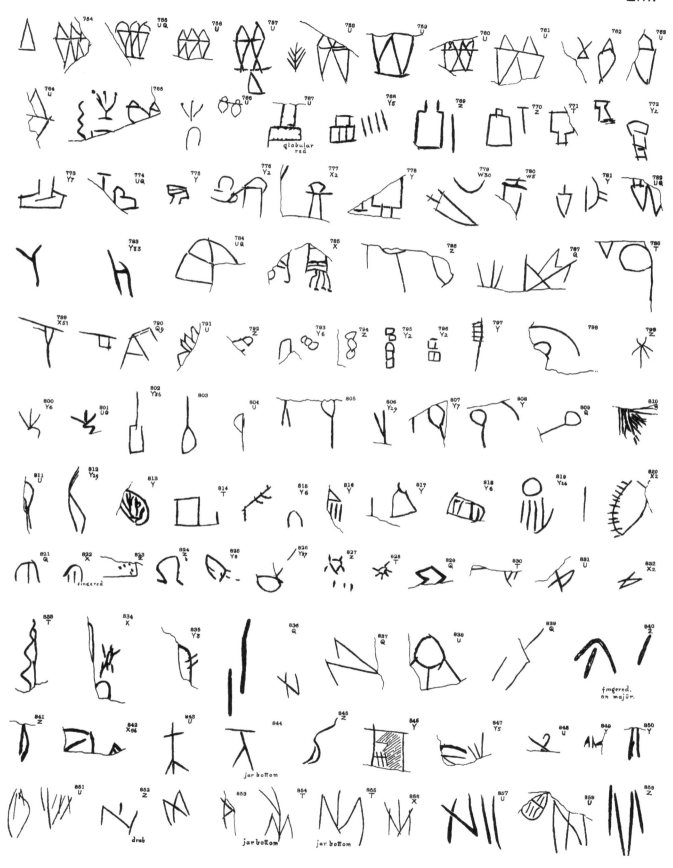

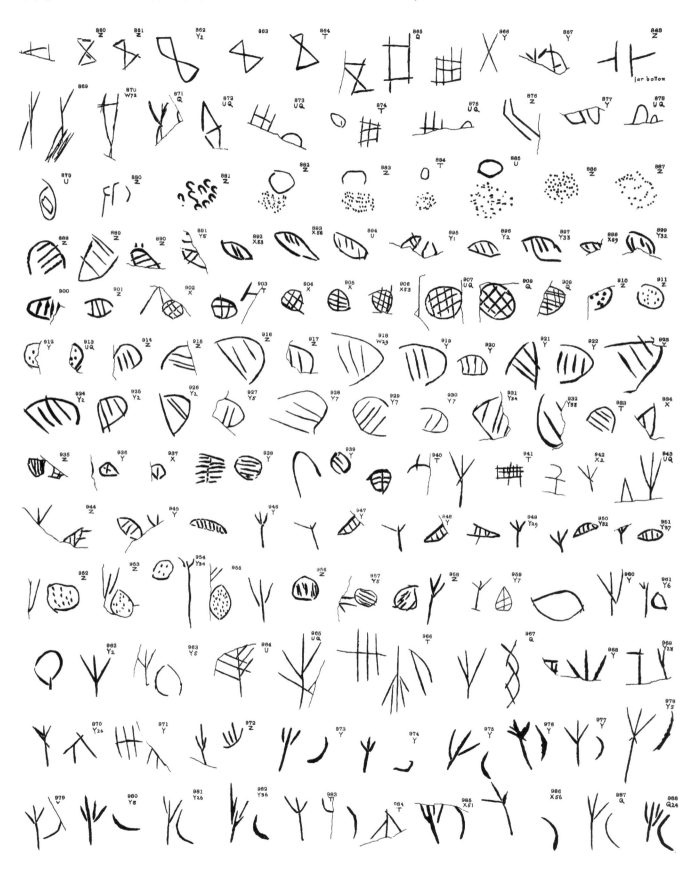

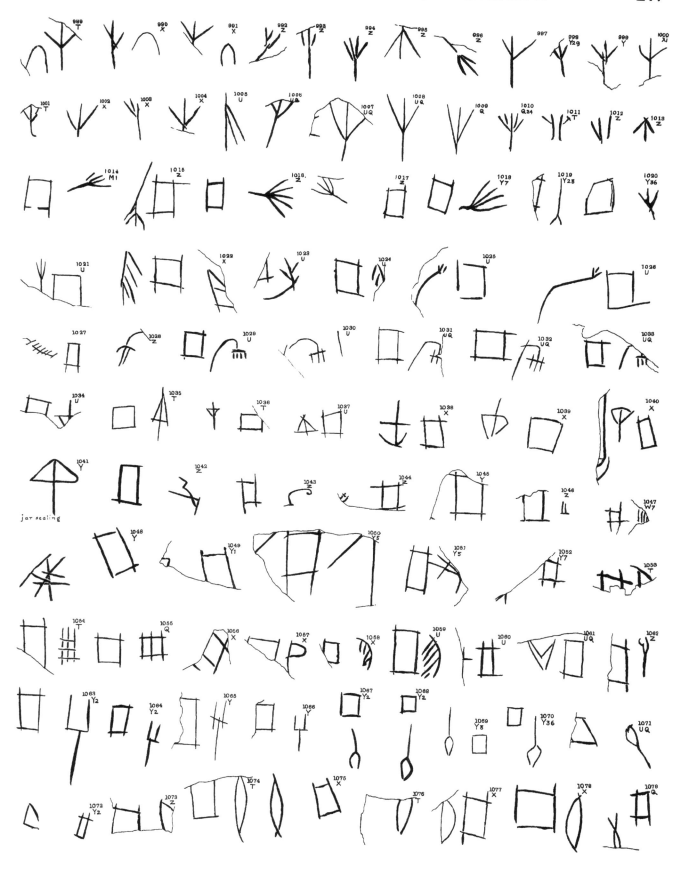

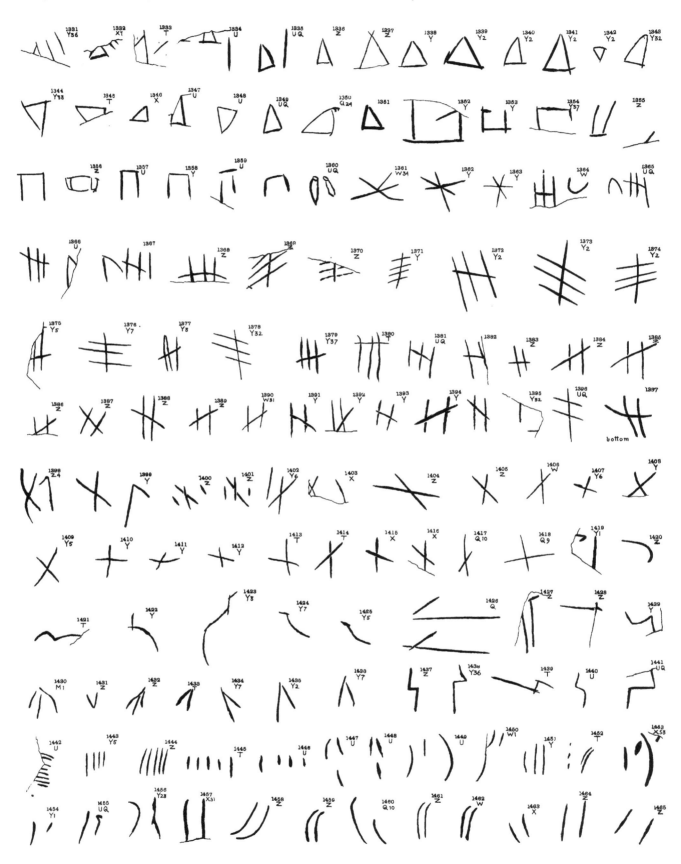

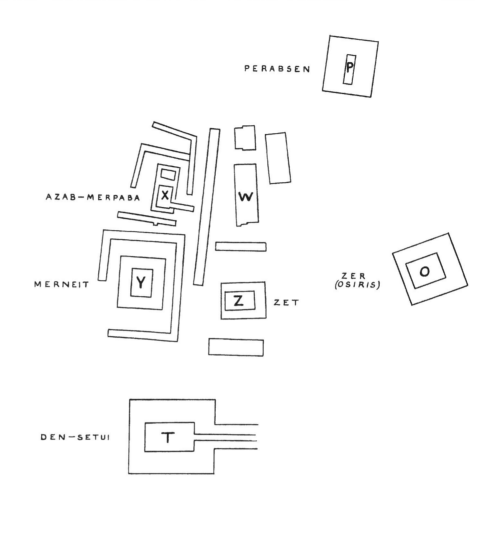

PERABSEN

AZAB—MERPABA

MERNEIT

ZET

ZER
(OSIRIS)

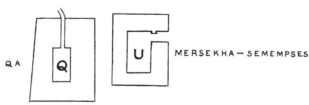

DEN—SETUI

QA

MERSEKHA—SEMEMPSES

KHA-SEKHEMUI

200 FEET

1:200 ABYDOS. TOMBS OF KINGS MERSEKHA-SEMEMPSES (U) & QA (Q). LX.

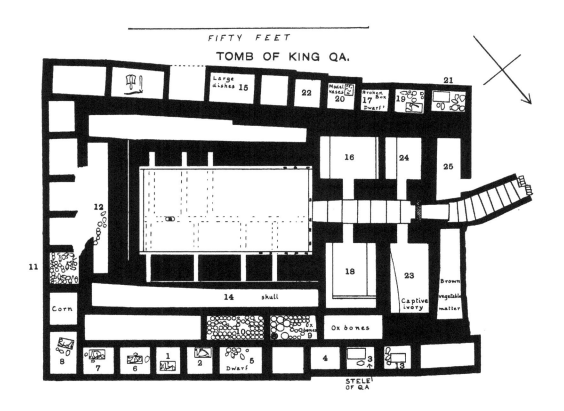

FIFTY FEET

TOMB OF KING QA.

Large dishes 15   22   Model vases 20   Broken Box 17 Dwarf?   19   21

16   24   25

12

11

Corn

14   skull

18   23   Captive ivory   Brown vegetable matter

Ox bones 9   Ox bones

8   7   6   1   2   Dwarf 5   4   3   13

STELE OF QA

TOMB OF KING MERSEKHA-SEMEMPSES.

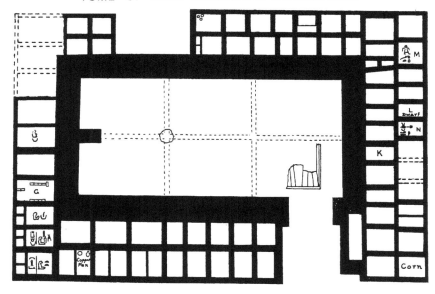

M

L Dwarf

N

K

G

A

Copper Pan

Corn

REMAINS OF WOODEN FLOOR
1:50

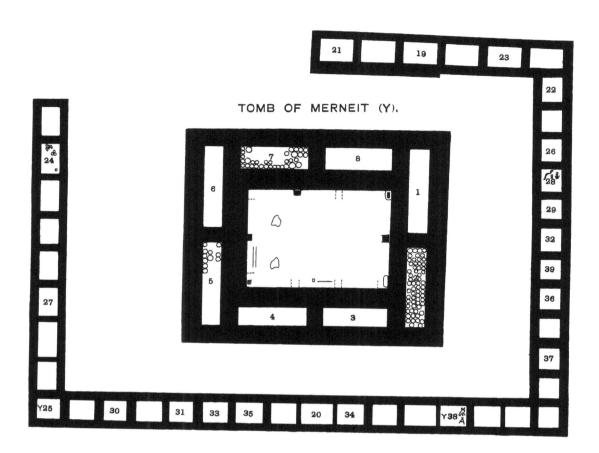

TOMB OF MERNEIT (Y).

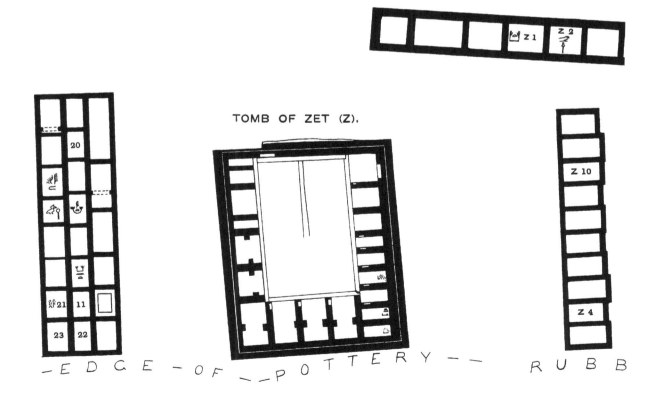

TOMB OF ZET (Z).

_E D G E _O F _ _P O T T E R Y _ _ R U B B

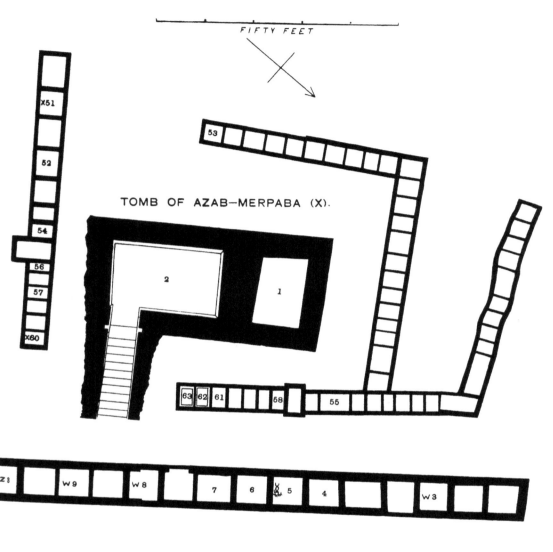

FIFTY FEET

TOMB OF AZAB—MERPABA (X).

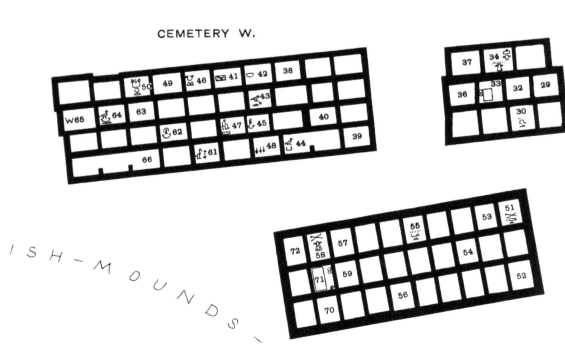

CEMETERY W.

ISH—MOUNDS

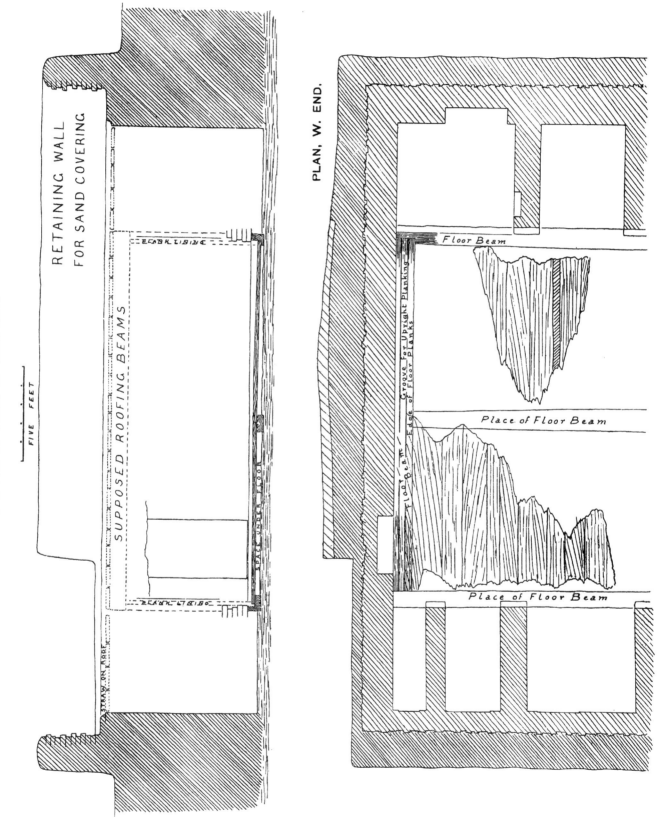

SECTION OF TOMB OF KING ZET.

FIVE FEET

RETAINING WALL FOR SAND COVERING

SUPPOSED ROOFING BEAMS

SPACE UNDER FLOOR

STRAW ON ROOF

PLAN, W. END.

Floor Beam

Place of Floor Beam

Place of Floor Beam

Groove for Upright Planking
Edge of Floor Planks
Floor Beam

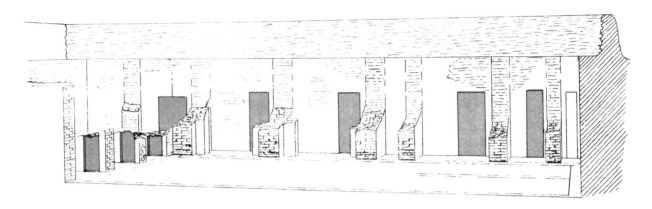

EAST END AND SOUTH WALL OF TOMB.

NORTH WALL OF TOMB,
SHEWING RECESSES COLOURED RED IN SIDE AND CROSS WALLS.

1 : 8   NAMES PAINTED ON SOUTH WALLS OF PRIVATE GRAVES.

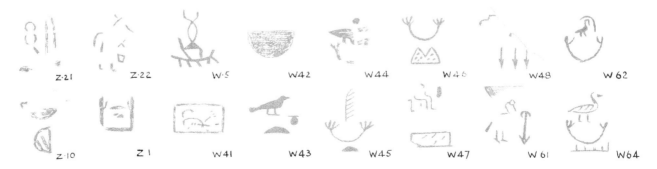

Z·21   Z·22   W·5   W42   W44   W46   W48   W 62

Z·10   Z I   W41   W43   W45   W47   W 61   W64

1.   TOMB OF ZET, LOOKING EAST.
                Chamber
                with Jars.

2.   TOMB OF ZET, N.W. CORNER.
             Plastered on Chamber sides.
             Rough Brick Retaining Wall above.

3.   TOMB OF ZET, LOOKING WEST.
   Recess.   N.W. Corner.

4.   TOMB OF ZET, LOOKING WEST.
          Shewing Beams and Planks of Floor.

5.   TOMB OF MERNEIT, LOOKING NORTH.
        Shewing part of Pilaster, and traces on wall.

6.   TOMB OF MERNEIT, LOOKING EAST.
             With back of defaced Stele.

SECTION OF TOMB OF KING MERNEIT.

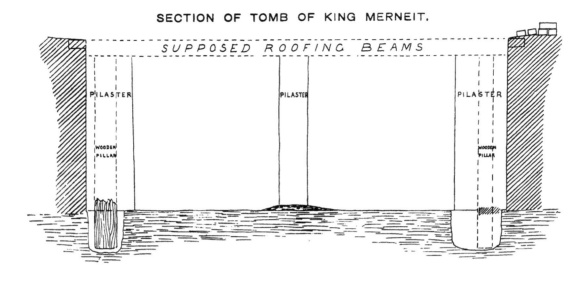

SECTION OF TOMB OF KING AZAB-MERPABA.

FIVE FEET

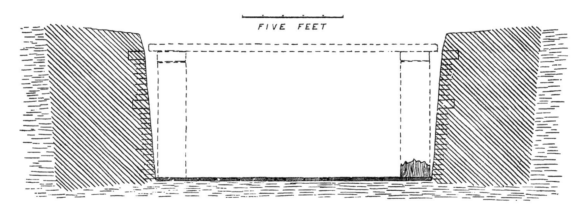

PLAN. N. END OF TOMB OF KING AZAB-MERPABA.

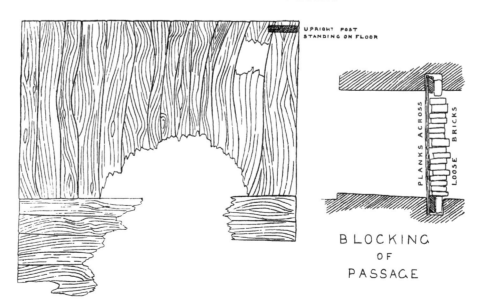

BLOCKING
OF
PASSAGE

1.   TOMB OF AZAB, LOOKING NORTH.
Shewing Wooden Floor and Side of Entrance.

2.   TOMB OF AZAB, ENTRANCE STAIRWAY.
Shewing Grooves and Blocking of Doorway.

3.   TOMB OF MERSEKHA, LOOKING SOUTH.
Shewing Pilaster.

4.   TOMB OF MERSEKHA, LOOKING EAST.
Shewing Wood Floor and Doorway.

5.   TOMB OF QA, LOOKING NORTH.
Shewing Doorway and Flooring Beams.

6.   TOMB OF QA, N.W. CORNER.
Shewing Flooring Beams and Stumps of Posts.

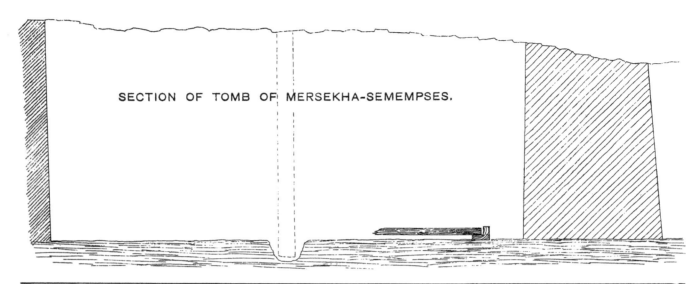

SECTION OF TOMB OF MERSEKHA-SEMEMPSES.

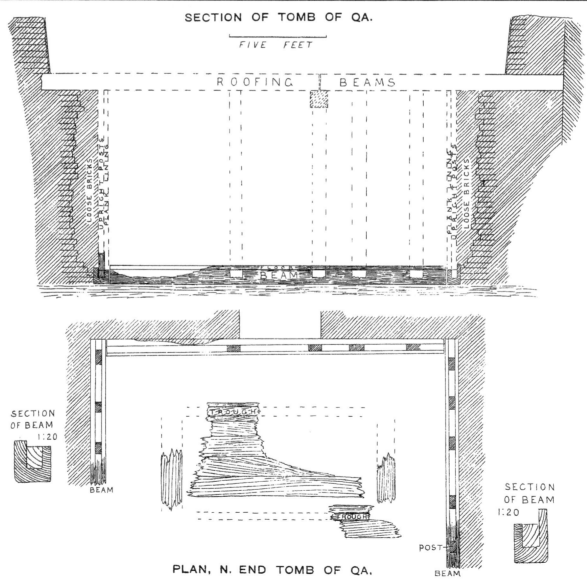

SECTION OF TOMB OF QA.

FIVE FEET

ROOFING BEAMS

LOOSE BRICKS

UPRIGHT POSTS
PLANK LINING

PLANK LINING
UPRIGHT POSTS
LOOSE BRICKS

FLOOR BEAM

SECTION OF BEAM 1:20

BEAM

TROUGH

TROUGH

POST

BEAM

SECTION OF BEAM 1:20

PLAN, N. END TOMB OF QA.